The California Consumer Privacy Act (CCPA)

An implementation guide

The California Consumer Privacy Act (CCPA)

An implementation guide

PRESTON BUKATY

IT Governance Publishing

Gianlori Pietroboy

Every possible effort has been made to ensure that the information contained in this book is accurate at the time of going to press, and the publisher and the author cannot accept responsibility for any errors or omissions, however caused. Any opinions expressed in this book are those of the author, not the publisher. Websites identified are for reference only, not endorsement, and any website visits are at the reader's own risk. No responsibility for loss or damage occasioned to any person acting, or refraining from action, as a result of the material in this publication can be accepted by the publisher or the author.

Apart from any fair dealing for the purposes of research or private study, or criticism or review, as permitted under the Copyright, Designs and Patents Act 1988, this publication may only be reproduced, stored or transmitted, in any form, or by any means, with the prior permission in writing of the publisher or, in the case of reprographic reproduction, in accordance with the terms of licences issued by the Copyright Licensing Agency. Enquiries concerning reproduction outside those terms should be sent to the publisher at the following address:

IT Governance Publishing Ltd
Unit 3, Clive Court
Bartholomew's Walk
Cambridgeshire Business Park
Ely, Cambridgeshire
CB7 4EA
United Kingdom
www.itgovernancepublishing.co.uk

The author has asserted the rights of the author under the Copyright, Designs and Patents Act, 1988, to be identified as the author of this work.

First published in the United Kingdom in 2019 by IT Governance Publishing.

ISBN 978-1-78778-132-0

ABOUT THE AUTHOR

Preston Bukaty is an attorney and consultant working for IT Governance USA. He specializes in data privacy GRC projects, from data inventory audits to gap analyses, contract management, and remediation planning. His compliance background and experience operationalizing compliance in a variety of industries give him a strong understanding of the legal issues presented by international regulatory frameworks. Having conducted more than 3,000 data mapping audits, he also understands the practical realities of project management in operationalizing compliance initiatives.

Preston's legal experience and enthusiasm for technology make him uniquely suited to understanding the business impact of privacy regulations such as the General Data Protection Regulation (GDPR) and the California Consumer Privacy Act (CCPA). He has advised more than 250 organizations engaged in businesses as varied as SaaS platforms, mobile geolocation applications, GNSS/telematics tools, financial institutions, fleet management software, architectural/engineering design systems, and web hosting. He also teaches certification courses on GDPR compliance and ISO 27001 implementation, and writes on data privacy law topics.

Preston lives in Denver, Colorado. Prior to working as a data privacy consultant, he worked for an international GPS software company, advising business areas on compliance issues across 140 countries. Preston holds a juris doctorate from the University of Kansas School of Law, along with a basketball signed by Hall of Fame coach Bill Self.

CONTENTS

Contents

INTRODUCTION

The lack of comprehensive privacy regulation in the US presents a unique set of compliance challenges for companies that collect personal data. Although a patchwork of sector-specific and state laws exist, they rarely deal with the pervasive collection and sale of people's personal information. Penalties for data breaches attempt to protect personal information by punishing companies for after-the-fact violations, but this does little to safeguard information in real time.

Ultimately, the issue is that data peddling is so pervasive. In the 2000s, Internet service companies such as Facebook and Google began collecting vast troves of personal data in an effort to personalize their online offerings. Search engines, for example, could consistently return better search results if user input and activity was analyzed. Social media networks, in contrast, tugged at innate human drives to connect and share with each other, which instilled a desire to maintain increasingly curated online profiles filled with personal details. Over time, these companies were able to monetize this information by using increasingly complex technologies that broadened the scale and complexity of data gathering to create detailed informational profiles on a person. Someone's interests, their income, political preference, or location – all could be used to tweak and sell ads targeted directly at that individual.

Marketers were willing to pay for access to this data, and so companies such as Facebook and Google profited immensely during the mid-to-late 2000s under a relative lack of regulatory oversight. Most consumers did not really grasp the technology behind this "surveillance capitalism," and often failed to realize just how vast the data collection network had grown. The technology companies were partly to blame – in amassing their fortune they employed a growing number of lobbyists at the state and federal levels to support their business model. So, for a long time, the issue went unresolved but not unnoticed.

In 2012, "a team of experts at Obama's Commerce Department worked on drafting a detailed privacy bill," but the proposal was "robbed [...] of both momentum and moral authority" by the revelations of Edward Snowden.[1] Snowden, "a former contractor for the National Security Agency, [...] revealed how the N.S.A. was collecting rivers of personal data — emails, photos, instant-message conversations — from nine leading internet companies, including Google, Facebook, Yahoo and Microsoft."[2]

Around this time, Alastair Mactaggart, a San Francisco-based real estate developer, began thinking about these rivers of personal data. He discovered that, "The rules [...] were largely established by the very companies that most relied on your data, in privacy policies and end-user agreements most people never actually read."[3]

---

[1] Nicholas Confessore, "The Unlikely Activists Who Took On Silicon Valley—and Won", August 2018, www.nytimes.com/2018/08/14/magazine/facebook-google-privacy-data.html.

[2] Ibid.

[3] Ibid.

Introduction

In response, Mactaggart hired a team of consultants to help draft and propose a new privacy bill for California – something aimed directly at the surveillance capitalists, attempting to restore a semblance of balance between the tech titans, their customers (marketers), and their products (average people). What came about was a ballot initiative that expanded the definition of personal data, granted a set of rights to consumers (access, deletion, opt-out) akin to European legislation, and a private right of action that expanded enforcement powers to all end users.

The Consumer Right to Privacy Act of 2018

Mactaggart's original ballot initiative included several key provisions. Most notably, it broadened the definition of "personal information" to contemplate new technologies and cover a variety of increasingly complex (and profitable) data elements. It also included a private right of action that enabled the law to be enforced by actual consumers whose rights were violated (in addition to California's attorney general).

Naturally, tech companies were antithetical to any proposed legislation that would curtail the influx of income earned from the unregulated collection and sale of such information. Business advocates in California also feared the expanded enforcement rights, which created an unknown, potentially huge litigation liability. They feared the cost of fighting vast numbers of private actions would deter businesses from operating in California, or even increase the cost of services for consumers. Thus, the ballot initiative met with strong opposition from government and industry, and it seemed unlikely the measure would pass in its original form. That is, until the Cambridge Analytica scandal of 2018.

3

In March 2018, Facebook quietly announced "it was suspending a political analytics firm called Cambridge Analytica from its platform after it had 'received reports' that Cambridge had improperly obtained and held data about Facebook users."[4] What followed was an onslaught of investigative reporting that revealed, "a contractor for Cambridge had harvested private information from more than 50 million Facebook users, exploiting the social-media activity of a huge swath of the American electorate and potentially violating United States election laws."[5] Public outrage ensued, and suddenly Mactaggart's proposal swarmed with enough support to overwhelm government and industry opposition. It seemed that if companies were unable or unwilling to regulate their collection and use of personal information, the voters of California would force them to do so.

AB-375

In response, the California legislature rushed to draft something that would effectively enforce privacy rights and also protect the business interests of their multi-billion-dollar constituents. AB-375 was signed on June 21, 2018, and California's governor signed on June 28. The new law

---

[4] Nicholas Confessore, "The Unlikely Activists Who Took On Silicon Valley—and Won", August 2018, *www.nytimes.com/2018/08/14/magazine/facebook-google-privacy-data.html*.

[5] Ibid.

expanded on some things previously unmentioned by Mactaggart's proposal, but it also changed some details.

For example, AB-375 required businesses to disclose categories and specific pieces of information collected about California consumers, as well as the business reason for collecting or selling that information, and the categories of third parties that receive it. It also prohibited the sale of personal information related to a consumer under the age of 16 without explicit (i.e. opt-in) consent.

Most notably though, AB-375 removed the consumer enforcement mechanism by gutting the private right of action found in Mactaggart's proposal. The new law conferred exclusive enforcement authority to California's attorney general for most provisions.[6] Consumers were left with a limited right to enforce paltry statutory penalties (in addition to actual damages) in the event of a data breach – $100 to $750 for:

> Any consumer whose nonencrypted or nonredacted personal information ... is subject to an unauthorized access and exfiltration, theft, or disclosure as a result of the business' violation of the duty to implement and maintain reasonable security procedures and practices appropriate to the nature of the information to protect the personal information.[7]

---

[6] AB-375 § 1798.150(c).

[7] AB-375 § 1798.150(a)(1).

Unfortunately, the enforcement mechanism was complex. Basically, a consumer was required to first provide 30 days' written notice to the business, identifying specific statutory violations.[8] If a business cured the violation within 30 days, "no action for individual statutory damages or class-wide statutory damages may be initiated against the business."[9] Only if the business continued to violate the statute, in breach of the express written statement provided, could the consumer initiate an action against the business for breach of that statement (along with any other privacy act violation).[10]

In addition, consumers were required to notify the attorney general within 30 days of an action being filed.[11] The attorney general was to then notify the consumer of an intent to bring enforcement action, or let the 30 days lapse and let the consumer proceed with the action.[12] Needless to say, AB-375 needed some clarification.

SB-1121

On August 31, 2018, the California State Legislature passed SB-1121, amending provisions of AB-375 to address

---

[8] AB-375 § 1798.150(b).

[9] AB-375 § 1798.150(b)(1).

[10] Ibid.

[11] AB-375 § 1798.150(b)(2),(3).

[12] Ibid.

inconsistencies and help implement a more comprehensive consumer privacy act.[13] Among other things, SB-1121:

- Clarified what defines "personal information" to explain that the information must "identify, relate to, describe, or reasonably link, directly or indirectly, with a particular consumer or household"[14]
- Delayed attorney general enforcement until six months after publication of implementing regulations, or July 1, 2020, whichever comes first (the attorney general being responsible for drafting and adopting those implementing regulations)[15]
- Limited civil penalties to $2,500 for each violation, up to $7,500 for each intentional violation, and possible injunction for organizations that violate the law[16]
- Changed the private right of action to no longer require attorney general notification, but kept its scope limited to data breaches caused "as a result of the business's violation of the duty to implement and maintain

---

[13] *https://leginfo.legislature.ca.gov/faces/billTextClient.xhtml?bill_id=2 01720180SB1121*.

[14] SB 1121 § 1798.140(o)(1).

[15] CCPA § 1798.185(a),(c).

[16] CCPA § 1798.155(b).

reasonable security procedures and practices appropriate to the nature of the information"[17]

- Carved out exceptions for coverage under other, similar laws (e.g. the Health Insurance Portability and Accountability Act (HIPAA), or parts of the state's Constitution)[18]
- Required a business that collects personal information to disclose consumers' right to delete that information, with such notices to be provided in a reasonably accessible form (as opposed to the website or online privacy policy, which was originally the case)[19]

As is likely clear, the legislative evolution of this proposal-turned-initiative-turned-law is a bit complex, and requires careful reading to understand the actual requirements for organizations.

---

[17] SB 1121 § 1798.150(a)(1).

[18] SB 1121 § 1798.145(c).

[19] SB 1121 § 1798.105(b).

CHAPTER 1: CCPA JURISDICTION – TERRITORIAL

Relevant provisions of the California Civil Code that collectively make up the California Consumer Privacy Act (CCPA) consistently refer to the rights of consumers as they apply to a "business". For example, "A consumer shall have the right to request that a business that collects a consumer's personal information disclose to that consumer the categories and specific pieces of personal information the business has collected."[20] Or, "A consumer shall have the right to request that a business delete any personal information about the consumer which the business has collected from the consumer."[21] As a result, the law's applicability hinges on key definitions of a "business", and, like all laws, organizations will need to carefully review definitions and terms to determine which portions of the statute apply.

Although many legal instruments include key terms as part of introductory text, the definitions for terms found in the CCPA are less obviously located. Many key terms can be found in section 1798.140. For example, "business" is defined in section 1798.140(c) as:

(1) A sole proprietorship, partnership, limited liability company, corporation, association, or other legal entity that is organized or operated for the profit or financial benefit of its shareholders or other owners, that collects

---

[20] Cal. Civ. Code § 1798.100(a).

[21] Cal. Civ. Code § 1798.105(a).

consumers' personal information, or on the behalf of which such information is collected and that alone, or jointly with others, determines the purposes and means of the processing of consumers' personal information, that does business in the State of California, and that satisfies one or more of the following thresholds:

(A) Has annual gross revenues in excess of twenty-five million dollars ($25,000,000), as adjusted pursuant to paragraph (5) of subdivision (a) of Section 1798.185.

(B) Alone or in combination, annually buys, receives for the business's commercial purposes, sells, or shares for commercial purposes, alone or in combination, the personal information of 50,000 or more consumers, households, or devices.

(C) Derives 50 percent or more of its annual revenues from selling consumers' personal information.

(2) Any entity that controls or is controlled by a business, as defined in paragraph (1), and that shares common branding with the business. "Control" or "controlled" means ownership of, or the power to vote, more than 50 percent of the outstanding shares of any class of voting security of a business; control in any manner over the election of a majority of the directors, or of individuals exercising similar functions; or the power to exercise a controlling influence over the management of a company. "Common branding" means a shared name, servicemark, or trademark.

Unfortunately, although the definition is long, it is not necessarily easy to understand. In order to understand if the CCPA applies, an organization must first determine whether it does business in the State of California.

Although the CCPA does not elaborate on what it specifically means to "do business in the State of California," there is relevant case law that can provide guidance. First, courts will look for general personal jurisdiction, which relates to a court's authority to hear cases within its established geographic area.

Typically, an incorporated business entity will be subject to the general personal jurisdiction of its home state. This is generally considered to be the state of incorporation, and/or the place of principal business (i.e. its headquarters).[22] For many organizations, this will mean that they can be subject to the general jurisdiction of two states. For example, if a company is incorporated in Delaware and its headquarters is in California, both Delaware and California will have general jurisdiction over the company. Thus, any organization actually established in California – perhaps by virtue of registering with the Secretary of State, among other things – should consider itself subject to the general jurisdiction of California's courts. Also, if the organization maintains a physical presence in California, the law will most likely apply.

However, there remains a question of extraterritorial reach. The issue is whether California, as a sovereign state, can apply its laws and regulations to organizations based outside the state but operating within it. These situations are often complex, and critical distinctions in a case can rely on

---

[22] US Supreme Court, *Daimler AG v. Bauman et al.*, 571 U.S. ___ (2014). *www.supremecourt.gov/opinions/13pdf/11-965_1qm2.pdf.*

individual factual circumstances. What if a business is not operating within the physical confines of the state but maintains a limited amount of business connections with California consumers? Does this subject the actions of an organization based in one state to the sovereignty of another state's courts? If one organization can therefore be held accountable by multiple (possibly many) states all at once, how many business connections with a state are necessary for that state to establish jurisdiction? In particular, how many connections with California consumers are necessary for a California law to apply to an organization based in another state?

When US courts fail to establish general jurisdiction, they then look to specific jurisdiction. Specific jurisdiction relates to the amount of contacts that a defendant has with a state. The idea is that a court operating in one state may not have sufficient authority over an out-of-state defendant to claim general jurisdiction by virtue of geography, but, based on the actions of the defendant – either by working within the state or dealing with local residents – a sufficient level of contact is established to grant the local court jurisdiction over the out-of-state defendant.

Typically, the defendant must have "purposefully avail[ed] itself of the privilege of conducting activities within the forum State," or have purposefully directed its conduct into the court's state.[23] For example, if a defendant commits a crime in one particular state, that state court will have

---

[23] *J. McIntyre Machinery, Ltd. v. Nicastro*, 564 U.S. 873, 877 (2011) (plurality opinion) (quoting *Hanson v. Denckla*, 357 U.S. 235, 253 (1958)).

specific jurisdiction as it relates to the crime, regardless of where the defendant organization is based. Keep in mind that the organization will also be subject to the jurisdiction of the state where it is based, so in theory there is always at least one court to enforce rulings. The question, as mentioned earlier, ultimately relates to extraterritorial reach and the sovereignty of state laws under the US Constitution. It also relates to fairness. Defendants should not have the burden of having to appear in multiple state courts if the matter really does not relate to that state. Moreover, plaintiffs should not be able to sue defendants in multiple states if there is no basis (or need) for that court to enforce additional judgment.

Again, these situations are sometimes complex, and increasingly so in the modern business environment. Large organizations may operate across the country, and thus maintain contact with every state all at once. Because they operate at a national level, it may be difficult to determine which states may exercise jurisdiction over an action that was purposely directed at all states, but not any one in particular.

Consider a company that markets and sells products nationally, such as a customer relationship management (CRM) software vendor. Should that company be subject to the jurisdiction of all state courts (and thus possibly have to appear in all state courts) simply because a few people in each state bought the allegedly liable product? Probably not, as it would pose an unfair burden to the defendant, in addition to constitutional questions of state power. This issue also becomes especially important in the context of class-action lawsuits, where huge groups of plaintiffs can be built up across the country. Therefore, in order to establish specific jurisdiction, a court must consider whether the actions of the defendant establish a sufficient level of contact with that state.

So, what is a sufficient level of contact? The California Supreme Court attempted to answer this question in 2016. In *Bristol-Myers Squibb Co. v. Superior Court (Anderson)*, a group of plaintiffs, comprised mainly of non-California residents, sued the pharmaceutical company Bristol-Myers Squibb Company (BMS) over alleged health defects caused by its product, Plavix.[24] The issue was that these plaintiffs sued BMS in California for liabilities under California law, despite there being no real connection to California. "The nonresident plaintiffs did not allege that they obtained Plavix through California physicians or from any other California source; nor did they claim that they were injured by Plavix or were treated for their injuries in California."[25] So, was a California court capable of enforcing judgment on an organization (in addition to the court where the organization was based) over actions that did not take place in California? And perhaps more importantly, could a group of plaintiffs – most with no real connection to California – sue a company in California courts for actions that did not take place in California?

In answering these questions, the California Supreme Court applied a "sliding scale approach to specific jurisdiction."[26]

---

[24] *Bristol-Myers Squibb Co. v. Superior Court*, 377 P.3d 874 (Cal. 2016).

[25] *Bristol-Myers Squibb Co. v. Superior Court*, 582 U.S. ____, 2 (2017); citing 1 Cal. 5th 783, 790, 377 P.3d 874, 879 (2016).

[26] 1 Cal. 5th, at 806, 377 P. 3d, at 889.

With this approach, the defendant's range of contacts can be used to show the connection between the defendant and the state.[27] As a result, the majority determined that it could exercise specific jurisdiction over the plaintiffs' claims "based on a less direct connection between BMS's [activities in California] and plaintiffs' claims than might otherwise be required [due to] BMS's extensive contacts with California."[28] Similarities between claims of the group's California and non-California residents effectively allowed California to hear the claims of the whole group.[29]

As mentioned earlier, the implications of these sorts of interpretations become immensely important when considering class-action lawsuits. The Court's ruling in *Bristol-Myers Squibb* would potentially allow class-action plaintiffs to sue defendants in California courts for violations of California law, even though the violations did not occur in California.

Such an important and far-reaching decision did not go without notice, and later in 2016 the United States Supreme Court granted a petition for a writ of certiorari (i.e. judicial review) over the case. There, the Court described the "danger of the California approach":[30]

---

[27] 1 Cal. 5th, at 806, 377 P. 3d, at 889.

[28] Ibid.

[29] Id., at 803–806, 377 P. 3d, at 887–889.

[30] *Bristol-Myers Squibb Co. v. Superior Court of California*, 582 U.S. ___, 8 (2017).

The mere fact that other plaintiffs were prescribed, obtained, and ingested Plavix in California—and allegedly sustained the same injuries as did the nonresidents—does not allow the State to assert specific jurisdiction over the nonresidents' claims. As we have explained, "a defendant's relationship with a . . . third party, standing alone, is an insufficient basis for jurisdiction." *Walden*, 571 U. S., at ___ (slip op., at 8). This remains true even when third parties (here, the plaintiffs who reside in California) can bring claims similar to those brought by the nonresidents.

The Court explicitly noted that there must be "a connection between the forum and the specific claims at issue."[31] In this case, the relevant plaintiffs were non-California residents: "all the conduct giving rise to the nonresidents' claims occurred elsewhere," and the plaintiffs did not "claim to have suffered harm in that State. […] It follows that the California courts cannot claim specific jurisdiction."[32]

So, it may be interpreted that California laws will apply to an organization established outside the state based on specific personal jurisdiction if the plaintiffs at issue are California residents who claim to have suffered harm in the state. That is, if the claims at issue arise from the defendant's activities in the state. Of course, the laws will also apply if the organization is established in California (i.e. general

---

[31] *Bristol-Myers Squibb Co. v. Superior Court of California*, 582 U.S. ___, 8 (2017).

[32] *Bristol-Myers Squibb Co. v. Superior Court of California*, 582 U.S. ___, 9 (2017).

jurisdiction by virtue of physical presence). Therefore, whether a business is "doing business in the state of California" – and therefore whether the CCPA applies to an organization – hinges on whether the organization maintains a physical presence in the state, or the degree to which California residents suffer harm in the state.

It should be noted that the CCPA does not prevent an organization from collecting or selling a consumer's personal information "if every aspect of that commercial conduct takes place wholly outside of California."[33] This requires that:

- The business collected that information while the consumer was outside of California
- No part of the sale of the consumer's personal information occurred in California; and
- No personal information collected while the consumer was in California is sold. [34]

So, according to section 145, the CCPA does not apply to commercial conduct that takes place outside of California. That said, it is not permissible for an organization to store personal information about a consumer while that person is in California, and then collect that personal information when the consumer leaves.[35]

---

[33] Cal. Civ. Code § 1798.145 (a)(5).

[34] Cal. Civ. Code § 1798.145 (a)(6).

[35] Ibid.

CHAPTER 2: CCPA JURISDICTION – MATERIAL

As noted previously, the CCPA applies to a "business." Here, legislative guidance is a bit more direct. A "business" for the purposes of the CCPA is defined in section 1798.140(c)(1) as:

1. A sole proprietorship, partnership, limited liability company, corporation, association, or other legal entity
2. That is organized or operated for the profit or financial benefit of its shareholders or other owners
3. That collects consumers' personal information, or on the behalf of which such information is collected and that alone, or jointly with others, determines the purposes and means of the processing of consumers' personal information
4. That does business in the State of California.

Although this definition may seem obvious on its face, there are some things to consider. First, the law only applies to an organization operated for "the profit or financial benefit" of its owners. Therefore, in its current state, the law does not apply to nonprofit organizations.

Second, the law only applies to organizations that collect personal information, or those that determine the purposes and means of processing that information. Great attention will likely be paid to this provision, as the rights of consumers – and thus, the responsibility of an organization to comply – apply to organizations that either collect information or determine the purposes of processing. For third-party service providers that generally only process a subset of data for limited purposes (and often based on explicit instruction), service agreements, data processing agreements, or other contractual arrangements will be critical. Exactly which organization determines the purposes and means of processing personal information will be the organization directly responsible for compliance with the CCPA; others in the data supply chain will likely only be liable for their limited processing.

This framework is similar to the one established by Europe's General Data Protection Regulation (GDPR). There, a "controller" is defined as the organization which "determines the purposes and means of the processing of personal data."[36] The data controller is responsible for demonstrating compliance with the GDPR under Article 24. In contrast, the data processor, which "processes personal data on behalf of the controller," is generally responsible for assisting the controller in its compliance obligations.[37] Consequently, the data controller is responsible for managing data subject rights and responding to requests for information. The data processor, in turn, helps the controller facilitate those rights and responds to those requests based on how it processes data for the controller.

Lastly, the CCPA only applies to organizations that do business in the State of California. As explained in the previous section, an organization does business in the state if it is physically established there, or if its activities in the state

---

[36] GDPR, Article 4(7).

[37] GDPR, Article 28.

2: CCPA jurisdiction – material

cause such harm to California residents that a California court could fairly adjudicate their claims.

That said, the CCPA's material jurisdiction also involves a threshold analysis. Naturally, not all laws apply to all people, and the same can be true for organizations. The CCPA only applies to organizations that:

1. Have annual gross revenues in excess of twenty-five million dollars ($25,000,000); or
2. Annually buy, receive, sell, or share for commercial purposes the personal information of 50,000 or more consumers, households, or devices; or
3. Derive 50 percent or more of its annual revenues from selling consumers' personal information.[38]

Again, it is clear that the CCPA only applies to organizations engaged in a commercial enterprise. They must operate for a profit at minimum; and, unless it is a large organization, they must profit from the sale or sharing of data in some way.

Now, the question of subsidiaries and other controlled entities may naturally arise. Section 1798.140(c)(2) explains that the law applies to, "Any entity that controls or is controlled by a business, (defined above) and that shares common branding with the business."[39] "Control" or "controlled" means ownership of, or voting power over, more than 50 percent of the outstanding shares of any class

---

[38] Cal. Civ. Code § 1798.140(c)(1).

[39] Cal. Civ. Code § 1798.140(c)(2).

of voting security; control in any manner over the election of a majority of the directors or individuals exercising similar functions; or the power to exercise a controlling influence over the management of a company.[40] The question remains as to what degree of control is required to meet the definition of "control" here as it applies to the influence of company management or the election of a board majority. The more sway or command that an organization has, though, over management of its subsidiary company or election of its board, the more likely it will be found that if the organization must comply, the subsidiary must comply as well (regardless of whether, for example, the subsidiary has no connection to California).

Of course, the law will not apply to organizations already covered under existing similar requirements. For example, organizations that collect or process protected health information governed by the "privacy, security, and breach notification rules [...] established pursuant to the Health Insurance Portability and Accountability Act of 1996 (HIPAA) and the Health Information Technology for Economic and Clinical Health Act (HITECH)."[41]

One final consideration. The law applies to organizations that collect personal information, or those that determine the means and purposes of processing personal information. "Processing" is defined as "any operation or set of operations that are performed on personal data or on sets of personal

---

[40] Cal. Civ. Code § 1798.140(c)(2).

[41] Cal. Civ. Code § 1798.145(c)(1).

data, whether or not by automated means."[42] Accordingly, as the definition of "processing" is broad enough to literally include "any operation [...] performed on personal data," it should be noted that almost any activity that occurs with regards to personal data will likely fall under the definition of "processing," and thus subject an organization to compliance with the CCPA. This can include passive activities, including storage of data.

---

[42] Cal. Civ. Code § 1798.140(q).

CHAPTER 3: THE CCPA - KEY DEFINITIONS

As noted earlier, many of the key definitions of terms and phrases are found in section 1798.140 of the CCPA. Much like the definition of "business," the terms defined in section 140 may have novel interpretations requiring careful analysis to understand how they apply to organizations.

Personal information

To start, it should be noted that the CCPA's definition of covered "personal information" encompasses a wide range of technological data markers. The term includes information "that identifies, relates to, describes, is capable of being associated with, or could reasonably be linked, directly or indirectly, with a particular consumer or household."[43] The statute then provides a non-exhaustive list of examples, but there are a few important things to consider at the outset.

First, note what could possibly be considered "personal information" by virtue of the definition's construction. According to the statute, "'Personal information' means information"[44] – there are no qualifiers preceding the word "information," so the *types* of information are not necessarily

---

[43] Cal. Civ. Code § 1798.140(o)(1).

[44] Ibid.

limited to any particular format, such as electronic data or paper files. All types of information are at issue.

The definition continues. "'Personal information' means information that identifies, relates to, describes, is capable of being associated with, or could reasonably be linked, directly or indirectly, with a particular consumer or household."[45] This is incredibly broad.

This definition includes not only descriptive information that directly identifies a person, but also information that indirectly identifies them. This approach is also seen in Europe, where the GDPR defines personal data as any information that can directly or indirectly identify a natural person.[46] The idea is that some data on its own presents relatively little privacy risk to an individual, perhaps because the individual can only be truly identified based on substantial efforts to collect and combine the indirect information into something more cohesive. Consider the anonymized GPS coordinates of exercise fanatics who favor a certain smartwatch application. On its own, one set of anonymized GPS coordinates would do little to identify an individual user, let alone present a privacy risk.

However, this does not negate the inherent value of those indirect identifiers. As is often the case with technology, anything can be achieved with enough information. By collecting enough of those GPS datasets over time, one could effectively map the location and coordinates of all users. With relatively little additional information – for example, a

---

[45] Cal. Civ. Code § 1798.140(o)(1).

[46] GDPR, Article 4(1).

known location or timestamped activity – one can quite easily pinpoint precisely which user was exercising where, and when. It is not difficult to imagine scenarios in which individual users are directly identified by combining multiple indirect identifiers. Therefore, although indirect identifiers may offer little substantive value on their own, they can still present a risk to privacy in the aggregate.

Although the CCPA's use of direct and indirect identifiers mirrors the definition of personal data under the EU's GDPR, the CCPA goes further. Whereas the GDPR deals with information that "identifies" a person, the CCPA adds that personal information can include information that "relates to [...] is capable of being associated with, or could reasonably be linked" to a person.[47] How exactly this piece of the definition will be interpreted and applied remains to be seen, but it certainly pulls a much larger subset of data into the covered definition of "personal information." For example, what level of indirect data linkage is necessary for that data to be considered "personal information"? When does an indirect link to data become so indirect that the "personal" aspect is essentially lost? Again, much of this remains to be seen, and will likely be sorted out through various interpretations of case law at the state level.

The CCPA does not stop there however. The definition of "personal information" ends with the following phrase: "with a particular consumer or household."[48] What this means is that, unlike the GDPR, the CCPA does not apply solely to natural persons (wherever located). The CCPA

---

[47] Cal. Civ. Code § 1798.140(o)(1).

[48] Ibid.

applies to information – *any* information that relates to, describes, identifies, is linked to or associated with – a consumer *or* household.

Since "household" is not specifically defined in other sections of the CCPA, it remains to be seen exactly how broad the definition of personal information may be when considering household data. For example, would historical home price information fall within scope? On its own, home price information provides no real private information – it merely relates to the price of a commodity over time, and commodities are often bought and sold between numerous parties. However, the historical home price of a particular house, in conjunction with employee payroll information, may fall within scope, as the combined information not only relates to the economic situation of a particular person (the employee), but also their entire household (perhaps reasonable links can be made to other data elements that give insight into the economic situation of the family as a whole). In that case, the home price information may be included as covered "personal information," although again, the interpretation of "household" remains to be seen.

That said, the CCPA's drafters did include a non-exhaustive list of personal data elements that help outline the scope of coverage. To be clear, personal information *can include*, but is not limited to, the following types of data elements:[49]

- Identifiers such as a real name, alias, postal address, unique personal identifier, online identifier, Internet Protocol address, email address, account name, Social

---

[49] CCPA § 1798.140(o)(1)(A)–(K).

Security number, driver's license number, passport number, or other similar identifiers

- Any categories of personal information described in subdivision (e) of Section 1798.80 (which relates to customer records)
- Characteristics of protected classifications under California or federal law
- Commercial information, including records of personal property, products or services purchased, obtained, or considered, or other purchasing or consuming histories or tendencies
- Biometric information
- Internet or other electronic network activity information, including, but not limited to, browsing history, search history, and information regarding a consumer's interaction with an Internet website, application, or advertisement
- Geolocation data
- Audio, electronic, visual, thermal, olfactory, or similar information
- Professional or employment-related information
- Non-public education information
- Inferences drawn from any of the information identified to create a profile about a consumer reflecting the consumer's preferences, characteristics, psychological trends, predispositions, behavior, attitudes, intelligence, abilities, and aptitudes

Some key elements worthy of consideration:

- IP addresses are specifically enumerated
- Biometric information, called out in subsection (E), is defined elsewhere as:

   an individual's physiological, biological or behavioral characteristics, including an individual's deoxyribonucleic acid (DNA), that can be used, singly or in combination with each other or with other identifying data, to establish individual identity. Biometric information includes, but is not limited to, imagery of the iris, retina, fingerprint, face, hand, palm, vein patterns, and voice recordings, from which an identifier template, such as a faceprint, a minutiae template, or a voiceprint, can be extracted, and keystroke patterns or rhythms, gait patterns or rhythms, and sleep, health, or exercise data that contain identifying information.[50]

- Browsing history, search history, and other information regarding a consumer's interaction with a website are also considered
- Geolocation data is covered
- Audio information (i.e. recorded calls and voice prompts) are covered, as is "visual, thermal, olfactory, or similar information." So, perhaps smells are included as "personal information"?

---

[50] Cal. Civ. Code 1798.140(b).

- "Inferences drawn from any of the information identified [...] to create a profile about a consumer reflecting the consumer's preferences, characteristics, psychological trends, predispositions, behavior, attitudes, intelligence, abilities, and aptitudes." This one is particularly interesting, because often those inferences drawn from personal data to help create behavioral profiles of customer preference trends are formed based on intellectual property and other business trade secrets. The question remains as to whether covered entities will be required to simply provide the customer profile and treat that as "personal information," or also provide insight into the algorithms and mechanisms that create those profiles

Importantly, covered "personal information" does not include publicly available information. As a result, information that has already been manifestly made public may not fall within the scope of the CCPA. The idea is that the information is already public, so why work further to protect the privacy of public information? That said, it should be noted that the law states, "'Publicly available' does not mean biometric information collected by a business about a consumer without the consumer's knowledge."[51] In addition, "Information is not 'publicly available' if that data is used for a purpose that is not compatible with the purpose for which the data is maintained and made available."[52] For this

---

[51] Cal. Civ. Code § 1798.140(o)(2).

[52] Ibid.

reason, it can likely be assumed that in order for information to qualify as "public," and therefore not be subject to the provisions of the CCPA, that information must have been made public with the knowledge of the consumer, and the intended use must be in line with that use originally contemplated when the information was first made public.

Aggregate consumer information

Other definitions found in section 1798.140 are equally important when understanding the interplay between various sections of the CCPA and its overall applicability. Consider the definition of "aggregate consumer information":

> information that relates to a group or category of consumers, from which individual consumer identities have been removed, that is not linked or reasonably linkable to any consumer or household, including via a device.[53]

The definition goes on to explain that, "'Aggregate consumer information' does not mean one or more individual consumer records that have been deidentified."

Two things are important with regards to this particular definition. First, it is vital for an organization to understand what constitutes "aggregate consumer information," because that dictates overall applicability of the law. Elsewhere in the legislation, section 145 of the Act makes clear that, "The obligations imposed on businesses by this title shall not restrict a business's ability" to do certain things, including

---

[53] Cal. Civ. Code § 1798.140(a).

common sense obligations such as complying with other laws or cooperating with law enforcement agencies.[54] It also does not prevent an organization from collecting or selling a consumer's personal information "if every aspect of that commercial conduct takes place wholly outside of California."[55]

Yet the section explains one final set of activities that the CCPA cannot restrict: the collection, use, retention, storage, or disclosure of consumer information that is either deidentified or in the aggregate.[56] So, the definition of "aggregate consumer information" is paramount. For example, large-scale marketing analytics, which typically provide substantial business value and are often sold at a corresponding price, may constitute "aggregate consumer information" and thus not be subject to the requirements of the CCPA.

Essentially, aggregate information is information about a group, with individual consumer identities removed. As a result, the information is not linked or linkable to any one particular consumer (or household). Rather, the information should be linked/linkable to the group at large – more akin to a single, conglomerate mass of anonymous individuals.

---

[54] Cal. Civ. Code § 1798.145(a)(1)–(4).

[55] Cal. Civ. Code § 1798.145(a)(5).

[56] Ibid.

Pseudonymization and deidentification

Interestingly, "anonymous" and "anonymize" are not defined in the CCPA. However, "pseudonymize" is, and it is markedly different from the definition of deidentified data. Remember, the CCPA does not restrict the collection, use, retention, storage, or disclosure of consumer information that is either deidentified or in the aggregate.[57]

"Deidentified" is defined as information that cannot "reasonably identify, relate to, describe, be capable of being associated with, or be linked, directly or indirectly, to a particular consumer."[58] In addition, the organization must have implemented both technical safeguards and business processes that prohibit reidentification of the consumer, while also making no further attempt on its own to reidentify the information.[59] The organization must also implement business processes to prevent the inadvertent release of the deidentified information – presumably as it applies to both systems specifically and general awareness training.[60]

In contrast, "pseudonymize" is defined as a process that "renders the personal information no longer attributable to a specific consumer without the use of additional information."[61] The difference is that deidentified data

---

[57] Cal. Civ. Code § 1798.145.

[58] Cal. Civ. Code § 1798.140(h).

[59] Ibid.

[60] Ibid. at (h)(3).

[61] Cal. Civ. Code § 1798.140(r).

3: The CCPA – key definitions

cannot be linked to a particular consumer – it is incapable of even being associated with that consumer – whereas pseudonymized data is no longer attributable without additional information. It can be reidentified, whereas deidentified data has been totally stripped of its identifying characteristics.

Granted, the process of pseudonymization, or separating information from its personal attributes, requires some additional steps, much like deidentification. Here, the organization is required to keep this additional attributing information separate from the pseudonymized set, and the additional information must be subject to both technical and organizational measures that ensure attribution (i.e. identification) does not take place.[62]

Pseudonymized data might look something like this:

Table 1: Pseudonymized Data

Customer	Expenses Q1	Expenses Q2	Expenses Q3	Expenses Q4
A	$348	$297	$190	$410
B	$72	$89	$90	$101
C	$149	$120	$133	$122
D	$301	$411	$295	$400

---

[62] Cal. Civ. Code § 1798.140(r).

In this instance, there would be a separate data set held elsewhere with identifying information linked to the customer alias, such as the customer's name, address, and billing information. Because the data above cannot be linked to a specific consumer or household without that additional information, the data is successfully pseudonymized. Deidentified data, however, would have no access to data that would identify the customers.

Collects, collected, collection

"Collects", "collected" or "collection" refer to the "buying, renting, gathering, obtaining, receiving, or accessing any personal information pertaining to a consumer <u>by any means</u>" (emphasis added).[63] This includes, "receiving information from the consumer, either actively or passively, or by observing the consumer's behavior."[64]

Consumer

"Consumer" means a natural person who is a California resident.[65] "Resident" is defined in the California Code of Regulations as every individual in the state for "other than a temporary or transitory purpose," and those who are domiciled in the state who may only leave for a temporary

---

[63] Cal. Civ. Code § 1798.140(e).

[64] Ibid.

[65] Cal. Civ. Code § 1798.140(g).

purpose.[66] "Natural persons" also typically refers to a human being, as opposed to a "legal person" (e.g. LLC entity).

Device

Many provisions of the statute deal with the collection or processing of data via a "device" of some kind. This is generally defined as, "any physical object that is capable of connecting to the Internet, directly or indirectly, or to another device."[67]

Homepage

"Homepage" means the introductory page of an Internet Web site and any Internet Web page where personal information is collected."[68] This definition will become important when discussing the rights of consumers, and how to facilitate those rights.

Person

"Person" means an individual, proprietorship, firm, partnership, joint venture, syndicate, business trust, company, corporation, limited liability company, association, committee, and any other organization or group of persons acting in concert."[69] Note that rights in relation to

---

[66] 18 CCR § 17014 (2017).

[67] Cal. Civ. Code § 1798.140(j).

[68] Cal. Civ. Code § 1798.140(l).

[69] Cal. Civ. Code § 1798.140(n).

data apply to consumers, not to persons. A "person" under the CCPA is not the equivalent of a "data subject" under the GDPR.

Research

Research with personal information collected during the course of a consumer's interactions with a business or device is subject to certain requirements.[70] Generally though, "research" is understood in the context of academic research, and not merely internal research and development processes devoted to product development or customer engagement. "Research," as defined here, "means scientific, systematic study and observation, including [...] research that is in the public interest and that adheres to all other applicable ethics and privacy laws or studies conducted in the public interest in the area of public health."[71]

Sell, selling, sale, sold

This is defined as the dissemination, disclosure, release, transfer, or other communication (oral or in writing), of a consumer's personal information for money or other valuable consideration.[72] Conversely, a business does not sell personal information when:[73]

---

[70] Cal. Civ. Code § 1798.140(s).

[71] Ibid.

[72] Cal. Civ. Code § 1798.140(t)(1).

[73] Cal. Civ. Code § 1798.140(t)(2)(A)–(D).

3: The CCPA – key definitions

- A consumer directs the business to intentionally disclose personal information, or uses the business to intentionally interact with a third party
- The business uses or shares a consumer identifier to alert third parties that the consumer has opted out of the sale of their personal information
- The business uses or shares personal information with a service provider because it is necessary to perform a business purpose, as long as the business notifies the consumer of the intended use, and the service provider does not further process the personal information (except as necessary to perform the original business purpose)
- The business transfers the information as part of a merger, acquisition, bankruptcy, or other transaction, as long as the processing of the information continues in a manner consistent with descriptions of processing given to the consumer when the personal information was originally collected

Third party

"Third party" means a person who is not one of the following:

- A business that collects personal information from consumers[74]

---

[74] Cal. Civ. Code § 1798.140(w)(1).

- A service provider[75]

Unique personal identifier

"Unique personal identifiers"[76] are listed as a category of "identifiers" in the definition of covered "personal information."[77] "Unique personal identifiers" are defined as, "a persistent identifier that can be used to recognize a consumer, a family, or a device that is linked to a consumer or family, over time and across different services."[78] Much like the definition of "personal information," the definition of "unique personal identifier" includes a non-exhaustive list of examples, including:

- A device identifier
- An Internet Protocol (IP) address
- Cookies, beacons, pixel tags, mobile ad identifiers, or similar technology
- Customer number, unique pseudonym, or user alias
- Telephone numbers
- Or other forms of persistent or probabilistic identifiers that can be used to identify a particular consumer or device

---

[75] Cal. Civ. Code § 1798.140(w)(2)(A).

[76] Cal. Civ. Code § 1798.140(x).

[77] Cal. Civ. Code § 1798.140(o)(1)(A).

[78] Cal. Civ. Code § 1798.140(x).

Now, some things to consider. First, as noted elsewhere, the amount of information covered by the CCPA's definition of "personal information" explicitly includes a wide range of technological markers. In contrast, Europe's GDPR points out in recital 30 that, "online identifiers provided by their devices, applications, tools and protocols [...] may leave traces" that, when combined, can be used to create profiles that identify someone.[79] However, recitals of the GDPR are only meant to provide additional guidance, and they do not serve as actual statute. As a result, nowhere in the actual blackletter law of the GDPR is mention made of things such as IP addresses or mobile ad identifiers. "Personal data" is merely defined as information relating to a data subject. Yet, some EU courts have interpreted that IP addresses constitute personal data.

The CCPA starts with a similarly broad definition of "personal information" – remember, the term includes information "that identifies, relates to, describes, is capable of being associated with, or could reasonably be linked, directly or indirectly, with a particular consumer or household."[80] Nevertheless, the list of enumerated examples provides a level of guidance directly iterated in statute. Unlike the GDPR's recitals, the CCPA explicitly provides a list of example technologies that constitute "unique personal identifiers," and thus covered "personal information," to help direct public thinking on this topic. A large range of data markers are specifically spelled out to ensure creative legal departments do not define terms narrowly enough to avoid

---

[79] GDPR, Recital 30.

[80] Cal. Civ. Code § 1798.140(o)(1).

jurisdiction. Regardless of how IP addresses or mobile ad identifiers are interpreted as "personal data" under the GDPR, it is clear that this information, and more, is covered by the CCPA.

Second, the CCPA includes "other forms of persistent or probabilistic identifiers that can be used to identify a particular consumer or device."[81] "'Probabilistic identifier' means the identification of a consumer or a device to a degree of certainty […] based on any categories of personal information included in, or similar to, the categories enumerated in the definition of personal information."[82] Under this definition, it could be argued that potentially any data marker that helps identify a consumer to a reasonable degree of certainty is considered a "probabilistic identifier", which constitutes a "unique personal identifier", which constitutes covered "personal information."

Verifiable consumer request

This definition is critical because an organization is generally only obliged to respond to a consumer (i.e. give effect to their rights), "upon receipt of a verifiable consumer request."[83] So, in order to understand when an organization must reply to consumer requests – and thus how the

---

[81] Cal. Civ. Code § 1798.140(x).

[82] Cal. Civ. Code § 1798.140(p).

[83] Cal. Civ. Code § 1798.140(y).

organization should build its respective response processes – it must first understand what constitutes a consumer request.

First, a "verifiable consumer request" must be made by a consumer, by a consumer on behalf of their minor child, or by a person registered with the Secretary of State (i.e. a business) authorized by the consumer to act on their behalf.[84] At the same time, an organization is "not obligated to provide information to the consumer […] if the business cannot verify […] that the consumer making the request is the consumer about whom the business has collected information."[85]

The definition also refers to verification mechanisms made pursuant to paragraph (7) of subdivision (a) of Section 1798.185. This section basically explains that the attorney general will solicit public commentary on parts of the regulation, and in turn adopt further regulations to provide clarity on enforcement. Paragraph (7) specifically states that the attorney general will establish:

> rules and procedures […] to govern a business's determination that a request for information received by a consumer is a verifiable consumer request, including treating a request submitted through a password-protected account maintained by the consumer with the business while the consumer is logged into the account as a verifiable consumer request and providing a mechanism

---

[84] Cal. Civ. Code § 1798.140(y).

[85] Ibid.

for a consumer who does not maintain an account with the business to request information through the business's authentication of the consumer's identity [...][86]

So, currently there are no recommended mechanisms to verify whether an incoming request actually relates to the consumer at issue. The statute does provide some guidance – for example, if the customer submits a request through their official account portal while logged in – but there is relatively little guidance for organizations that do not maintain active account profiles for their users. Consequently, organizations will need to consider alternative verification mechanisms when handling consumer requests for information, keeping in mind that any additional data requested for verification purposes creates an additional compliance burden on this new set of data. It may be advisable then for organizations to consider creating dedicated account management portals to help end users effectively manage their own personal information within the organization's systems.

---

[86] Cal. Civ. Code § 1798.185(a)(7).

CHAPTER 4: ROLES IN THE CCPA: BUSINESSES, BUSINESS PURPOSE AND SERVICE PROVIDER

Considerable attention has already been given to what constitutes a "business" under the CCPA. As explained, "business" describes covered entities, those organizations primarily responsible for complying, and demonstrating compliance with the CCPA. This responsibility largely hinges on which organization in the data supply chain collects personal information, or directs the means and/or purposes for processing the information. This is similar to the GDPR's understanding of a "data controller."

Under the GDPR, there are both "data controllers" and "data processors." Data processors process personal information on behalf of the data controller, usually based on explicit instruction as outlined in a contract. This situation typically arises in the context of service providers that process data – CRM and enterprise resource planning (ERP) solutions, payroll providers, technology solutions (Cloud offerings, Software as a Service (SaaS), Platform as a Service (PaaS), Logging as a Service (LaaS), etc.). The CCPA sees things similarly, and actually uses the term "service providers" to describe those organizations "that process information on behalf of a business and to which the business discloses a consumer's personal information for a business purpose pursuant to a written contract."[87]

---

[87] Cal. Civ. Code § 1798.140(v).

Data processing contracts under the GDPR are governed by Article 28(3), and several things are specifically required. For example, contracts with data processors should include the obligation of confidentiality (i.e. a confidentiality agreement).[88] There must also be relevant security provisions pursuant to Article 32 (technical and organizational measures appropriate to the risk).[89] The CCPA, in contrast, provides relatively little in terms of defined contractual requirements.

The definition of "service provider" in paragraph (v) explains that the contract with said service provider must prohibit "the entity receiving the information from retaining, using, or disclosing the personal information for any purpose other than for the specific purpose of performing the services specified in the contract for the business." Of course, the service provider may be able to process the personal information for additional purposes outside those outlined in the contract, assuming that processing takes place in accordance with all relevant provisions of the CCPA.[90]

Because businesses can disclose a consumer's personal information to a service provider pursuant to a written contract based on a "business purpose," it is critical to understand what "business purpose" is. Disclosing personal information to an organization for something other than a

---

[88] GDPR Art. 28(3)(b.)

[89] Ibid. at (3)(c).

[90] Cal. Civ. Code § 1798.140(v).

"business purpose" may fall outside the remit of the CCPA's "business" and "service provider" distinction.

"Business purpose" generally includes internal, operational uses. Paragraph (d) outlines what "business purposes" actually are, according to statute.[91]

Business purposes are:

(1) Auditing related to a current interaction with the consumer and concurrent transactions, including, but not limited to, counting ad impressions to unique visitors, verifying positioning and quality of ad impressions, and auditing compliance with this specification and other standards.

(2) Detecting security incidents, protecting against malicious, deceptive, fraudulent, or illegal activity, and prosecuting those responsible for that activity.

(3) Debugging to identify and repair errors that impair existing intended functionality.

(4) Short-term, transient use, provided the personal information that is not disclosed to another third party and is not used to build a profile about a consumer or otherwise alter an individual consumer's experience outside the current interaction, including, but not limited to, the contextual customization of ads shown as part of the same interaction.

(5) Performing services on behalf of the business or service provider, including maintaining or servicing accounts,

---

[91] Cal. Civ. Code § 1798.140(d).

providing customer service, processing or fulfilling orders and transactions, verifying customer information, processing payments, providing financing, providing advertising or marketing services, providing analytic services, or providing similar services on behalf of the business or service provider.

(6) Undertaking internal research for technological development and demonstration.

(7) Undertaking activities to verify or maintain the quality or safety of a service or device that is owned, manufactured, manufactured for, or controlled by the business, and to improve, upgrade, or enhance the service or device that is owned, manufactured, manufactured for, or controlled by the business.

Note that this section of statute does not include the phrase "including, but not limited to." It follows that the list of "business purposes" provided in paragraph (d) is intended to serve as a complete and final list, as there is no carve-out for possible business purposes currently not under consideration.

In consequence, if any of these activities will be managed by an organization (a service provider) other than the original business, the business will need a contract in place that, at the very least, prohibits the service provider from processing the personal information for any purpose other than the purpose specifically outlined.

Naturally, both the business and service provider may wish to include other contract terms. For example, the entities could enforce a confidentiality agreement with regards to the personal information, akin to the GDPR. They may also

4: Roles in the CCPA: businesses, business purpose and
service provider

enforce security requirements on each other to help ensure
the processing of personal information does not subject any
one company to liability based on bad business practices. At
the very least, a data processing contract should include an
assurance from the service provider that it understands the
restrictions as outlined, and will comply with them.

CHAPTER 5: RIGHTS OF CONSUMERS AND OBLIGATIONS OF THE BUSINESS

The CCPA outlines several requirements that apply to a "business." Collectively, this is the operational impact of the CCPA. Although these are often listed as consumer rights, they also impose obligations on a business to allow consumers to exercise those rights.

There are three consumer rights:

1. Right of access – a right to have the business disclose various pieces of information related to the data processing[92]
2. Right to opt-out – a right to request that a business that sells personal information to third parties no longer sell the consumer's personal information[93]
3. Right to deletion – a right to request that the business delete certain personal information about the consumer that the business collected[94]

All of these rights take effect in various forms, and the obligations they impose on organizations may seem daunting at first glance. The key here is to understand what each of these rights requires of the organization and how these requirements overlap. With that understanding, the

---

[92] Cal. Civ. Code § 1798.100, 110, 115.

[93] Cal. Civ. Code § 1798.120.

[94] Cal. Civ. Code § 1798.105.

organization can develop reliable, repeatable processes for complying with the CCPA's requirements.

Right of access

This right is actually iterated in a few places throughout the CCPA. The first is at the outset – section 100: "A consumer shall have the right to request that a business that collects a consumer's personal information disclose to that consumer the categories and specific pieces of personal information the business has collected."[95] It is expanded in section 110:[96]

A consumer shall have the right to request that a business that collects personal information disclose the following:

- The categories of personal information it has collected about that consumer
- The categories of sources from which the personal information is collected
- The business or commercial purpose for collecting or selling personal information
- The categories of third parties with whom the business shares personal information
- The specific pieces of personal information it has collected about that consumer

---

[95] Cal. Civ. Code § 1798.100(a).

[96] Cal. Civ. Code § 1798.110(a), (1)–(5).

As noted earlier, this information must be disclosed to the consumer upon receipt of a verifiable consumer request.

In addition to responding to requests, any business that collects consumer personal information is required to inform consumers at the time of collection as to the categories of personal information to be collected and the purposes for which the information will be used.[97] Additional information cannot be used without providing consistent, similar notice. An easy way to help manage this obligation is simply explaining this information in the privacy notice, and linking or referring to this notice where data is collected.

Other requirements apply relative to the right of access when an organization sells consumers' personal information. These requirements can be found in section 115.

For example, upon receipt of a verifiable consumer request, a business that sells personal information must disclose to the consumer:[98]

- The categories of personal information that the business collected about the consumer
- The categories of personal information that the business sold about the consumer
- The categories of third parties to whom the personal information was sold (by category of personal information for each third party)

---

[97] Cal. Civ. Code § 1798.100(b).

[98] Cal. Civ. Code § 1798.115(a), (1)-(3).

- The categories of personal information that the business disclosed about the consumer for a business purpose

As can be seen, the requirements for organizations that sell personal information are substantially similar to those in sections 100 and 110, which detail the information that must be provided by organizations that simply collect personal information. In either case, organizations processing personal information should be prepared to respond to requests for information relating to the types of information listed above.

Responding to these types of requests will naturally require an innate understanding of an organization's IT infrastructure and business processes. Of course, the front-end parts of the organization that regularly deal with external parties will likely come into play. Marketing, sales, and customer support are usually some of the key business functions that regularly collect, store, share, or sell customers' personal information. These groups also often collect personal information related to sales agents, account managers, and other business contacts as part of their day-to-day work. Do not neglect this information, especially if those business contacts are California residents (i.e. consumers whose personal information is covered by the CCPA). This may depend on your industry though.

Organizations are often advised to focus on their front-end, external-facing processes and systems first, because these often present a greater risk to the organization than the internal-facing operations. Ideally, internal issues can be handled internally. In contrast, any external issues – a concerned customer or media contact – are more likely to be handled externally, either by a regulatory enforcement body (in this case, the California attorney general) or individual consumers in civil suit. Internal operations are just as important, however. Administrative functions traditionally managed by human resources (HR) or those in a management role, typically involve detailed personal information beyond contact identifiers – payroll information, health benefits information, bank accounts, names of spouses and/or children, calendar details, gender, race/ethnicity, criminal backgrounds, etc. This information deserves additional protection based on its sometimes more sensitive nature. That said, a healthy organization should have robust internal reporting mechanisms that handle any complaints efficiently, effectively, respectfully, and internally, before the issue can escalate externally.

Considering the potential operational impact of responding to consumer requests individually, mature organizations should consider a variety of mechanisms to help manage any increased workload related to incoming consumer requests. There are several options available.

Any organization that collects or sells personal information will have to comply with section 130 of the CCPA concerning the response to "right of access" requests. This section requires two things:

1. The organization must provide at least two designated methods that allow consumers to submit requests for information, "including, at a minimum, a toll-free

telephone number, and if the business maintains an Internet Web site, a Web site address."[99]

2. The organization must provide the required information to the consumer free of charge within 45 days of receiving the request.[100] Although the organization is required to "promptly take steps to determine whether the request is a verifiable consumer request," this does not affect the 45-day window.[101] Ultimately, the total time to respond is 45 days after receipt. This period may be extended once, by an additional 45 days, provided the consumer is given notice of the extension within the first 45-day period.[102]

For this reason, organizations need to prepare verification mechanisms and corresponding business processes that allow for quick and easy verification of consumer requests. Essentially, organizations need to ensure that the person submitting a request for information is actually the consumer who they claim to be. The importance of this should be obvious – hackers looking to surreptitiously steal personal data should not be able to merely ask for it. A level of authentication should occur. Each industry will also have differing requirements for authentication to protect consumers, clients, employees, partners, and business

---

[99] Cal. Civ. Code § 1798.130(a)(1).

[100] Cal. Civ. Code § 1798.130(a)(2).

[101] Ibid.

[102] Ibid.

interests. For example, legal services may regularly deal with aggrieved spouses looking for information on recent address changes. Alternatively, investment entities may need to protect geolocation data in case it provides insight on travel related to mergers and acquisitions. In any case, the organization at issue should consider the context of the industry within which it operates. This will help provide guidance on the relative level of authentication necessary to process and handle an incoming "right to access" request.

Organizations only have to provide information related to the past 12 months.[103] The response is to be made in writing, and delivered through either the consumer's account or at the consumer's option (again a compelling reason to consider creating a consumer account portal where requests for information can be collectively tracked and stored, although it should be noted that organizations cannot require a consumer to make an account in order to make a verifiable consumer request).[104] Organizations are also not obligated to reply to the same consumer request more than twice in a 12-month period.[105]

Curiously, there is wording buried in subparagraph (a)(2) of section 130 that contains language similar to the GDPR's "right to data portability." Article 20 of the GDPR states:

---

[103] Cal. Civ. Code § 1798.130(a)(2).

[104] Ibid.

[105] Cal. Civ. Code § 1798.130(b).

The data subject shall have the right to receive the personal data concerning him or her [...] in a structured, commonly used and machine-readable format and have the right to transmit those data to another controller without hindrance [...][106]

The CCPA, meanwhile, requires responses to verifiable consumer requests to be provided "in a readily useable format that allows the consumer to transmit this information from one entity to another entity without hindrance."[107] Considering this requirement applies to both categories and specific pieces of information, organizations must be able to respond completely to consumer requests, which means that they must be able to identify and gather the necessary information, and provide it to the consumer in the appropriate format.

This will likely require data mapping or data flow audits that help track what data is collected from consumers, how that data is used, and where it is stored. In turn, this will help personnel reply to verifiable consumer requests, because they will ideally have access to a controlled repository where they can quickly filter and search for key data elements related to a consumer, along with additional information related to the organization's use or intended business purpose for the data.

---

[106] GDPR, Article 20(1).

[107] Cal. Civ. Code § 1798.130(a)(2).

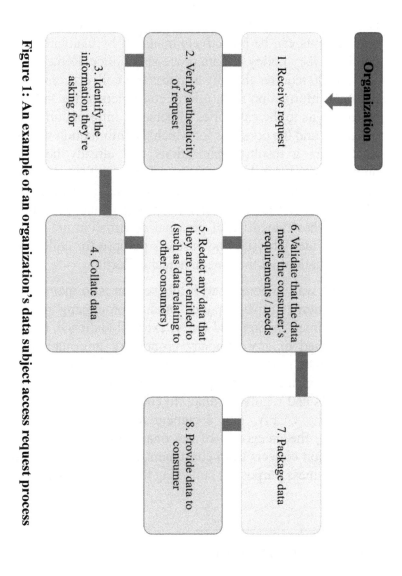

Figure 1: An example of an organization's data subject access request process

Data processing notices

Section 130 of the CCPA outlines some other obligations. As is likely imaginable, many of the aforementioned requirements can be proactively managed by maintaining a public privacy policy or data processing notice. Remember, section 100 requires that any business that collects consumer personal information must inform consumers at the time of collection as to the categories of personal information to be collected, and the purposes for which the information will be used.[108] As a result, organizations will already need to prepare some kind of public privacy policy or data processing notice based on the requirements in section 100. That is, any organization that collects personal data must explain what categories of personal information are being collected, and why (i.e. the business purpose for collecting the information), at the time of actual collection.

The ideal way to comply with this section is to maintain a single, external privacy policy or data processing notice. This document is prepared for an external audience, and is whitewashed of any company proprietary information or internal trade secrets. This is the document that gets posted to the organization's website; it is the document shared with consumers and regulators alike. In compliance with section 100 of the CCPA, this document should explain, at a minimum, the categories of personal information that an organization collects from consumers, and their operational use or business purpose in collecting that information.

---

[108] Cal. Civ. Code § 1798.100(b).

Section 100 makes clear that this document, or more generally, this notice of information to be collected, should be provided at or before the "point of collection" – that is, before the information is collected, or at the actual time of collection.[109] For example, some organizations may maintain a process whereby data is collected – an online form with static or dynamic data collection fields – which is when this privacy policy or data processing notice should be provided.

Data can, of course, be collected by other methods as well: paper forms, telephone calls, email outreach, etc. An organization may wish to prepare its data privacy notice in respect to specific data collection processes if each of those processes is sufficiently distinct enough to warrant a separate notice for each process. However, the actual management of those notices may start to become a burden onto itself. Collaborative authoring, version control, publishing authority, and other aspects of corporate communications will need to be managed for each individual policy document that describes the data processing activities at issue. For large organizations, this can easily create a cumbersome and unrealistic approach to managing notices and access.

Organizations have a variety of disclosure obligations as well, set out in sections 100, 110, and 115 of the CCPA. These disclosures are usually in response to a consumer request, but sometimes exist as general requirements. Ideally then, rather than maintaining separate processes focused on each individual aspect of compliance, organizations will consider a holistic approach to compliance – a programmatic model, as opposed to a "check-the-box" initiative. Again, it

---

[109] Cal. Civ. Code § 1798.100(b).

is important to understand each individual part of the CCPA to help fully grasp it as a whole.

A holistic approach to CCPA compliance will weave together various interrelated parts of the statute. In this case, these will be the requirements related to notice, disclosure, and access. Mature organizations will start to comply by first engaging in data mapping or data flow activities, to find out exactly what information they collect, for what purpose, and with whom that information may also be shared.

Once the full data lifecycle is understood internally, only then can it be explained externally. Ideally, this should be done in a single data privacy policy or processing notice. Rather than maintaining separate documents to describe separate data processing activities, organizations should aim to outline and explain their entire data processing model in a single document or series of documents (or at least as much as is appropriate for public consumption). This will help centralize coordination and control over this single "master document" that outlines all practices relevant to personal data and privacy. The master document can then be shared as necessary, ideally via a link, so that all personnel access and refer to the same source of truth as a matter of practice. This helps eliminate the confusion sometimes associated with document management in a corporate context – who made which revisions, whether a document is suitable for external release, what version is the correct version, etc. Where data is actually collected by the organization, subsequent web pages or forms can link to the original policy document, which should also live as a standalone page on the organization's web platform – usually under a commonly-used title, such as "Privacy" or "Privacy Policy," or "How we use your data."

From there, organizations will need to consider the format and structure of this policy document. The policy should be structured in a way that is not overly confusing to average consumers. That is, the document should be written clearly, with commonly used terms that minimize the use of industry slang or legal jargon. Statements that outline data processing practices should aim to provide clarity, with direct sentences that avoid unclear, qualifying language (e.g. "sometimes," "we may," "in certain circumstances"). Paragraphs and sentences should be appropriately grouped so that it is clear which products, services, or processes collect and process which personal information for which purposes. An average person should be able to readily navigate to the organization's privacy policy, read the policy with minimal issue or confusion, and walk away with a relatively clear understanding of what personal data processing looks like at the organization. Clearly, some time should be spent determining what exactly is included in this policy document. Some organizations may find it useful to look at publicly available privacy policies to get a sense of how others in their industry have approached the structure and format of the policy or notice.

The data privacy policy or data processing notice must include the following:

A description of consumer rights, pursuant to Sections 1798.110, 1798.115, and 1798.125.[110]

Often, organizations will choose to simply list those rights in their policy documents. Actual explanation of which consumer's rights apply in an individual scenario can be

---

[110] Cal. Civ. Code § 1798.130(a)(5)(A).

managed via the "verifiable consumer request" (i.e. outreach) mechanism.

A description of the method for submitting verifiable consumer requests.[111]

Typically, organizations will maintain a point-of-contact email address for handling issues related to data privacy, cybersecurity, and data governance. This email inbox may be managed by a single person, such as a data privacy officer or chief compliance officer. Alternatively, it may be handled by a team or department. The person or persons may just be responsible for responding to consumers, or they may also manage the entire privacy compliance program. The internal structure and associated processes are of less relevance at this stage; what is important is that the organization's privacy policy does maintain a point of communication, generally via email, whereby privacy issues and consumer privacy rights are managed. It should be enough that organizations outline the rights enumerated by the CCPA, and simply point consumers to the point of contact for more information or explanation of those rights. Do not forget though – the organization must make available, at a minimum, a toll-free telephone number – see section 130(a)(1) – so in reality, a CCPA privacy policy will include contact information for an organization's privacy manager in both email and telephone format.

---

[111] Cal. Civ. Code § 1798.130(a)(5)(A).

A list of categories of information and the purpose for which those categories will be used.[112]

This requirement to list categories of information collected comes from section 130, and relates to compliance with section 110(c), which also discusses the disclosure of specific pieces of personal information collected. Remember though, an organization that collects personal information is simultaneously subject to the requirements of section 100. As a result, in addition to listing the categories of information collected, organizations may wish to explain what specific pieces of information constitute those categories, likely in an effort to help consumers understand more clearly what data is at issue.

For guidance, consider the categorical groupings listed in section 140(o)(1): identifiers, protected classes, commercial information, biometric information, education information, employment information, location data, etc.

A list of categories of information that may be sold or disclosed for a business purpose.[113]

Organizations may wish to consider how this will be presented and explained in the privacy policy. Does it make sense to group data collection activities by product or service? What about activities involving the onward transfer of data? There is no correct approach here, and the final style used will depend largely on the organization and the complexity of its data processing activities. Ultimately though, the reader should not find it difficult to understand

---

[112] Cal. Civ. Code § 1798.100(b).

[113] Cal. Civ. Code § 1798.130(a)(5)(C).

what data is being collected, for what purpose, and who else may receive that data, whenever the customer uses the product or service at issue.

Note that as it applies to the policy document, the list of categories of personal information collected or sold applies only to the preceding 12 months.[114] Consequently, the organization is responsible for updating information contained in the policy at least once every 12 months.[115]

To manage this, organizations will need to consider review and revision processes for the policy. Senior management should be involved in an annual process to review the policy document itself, while stakeholders from various business functions should be allowed to inject input in real time. This allows any day-to-day changes to be captured immediately if they have a privacy impact, whereas other process changes that do not heavily impact privacy can be reviewed on a periodic basis. The review process should include change management methodologies to help ensure all relevant parties are aware of what has changed versus what has stayed the same. Invariably, the policy's publication date should be updated annually as well.

Considering the amount of information that must be included in an organization's privacy policy, and given the considerable back-end processes required to update and disseminate the policy, mature organizations should consider adding some extra information to their public-facing policies. This additional information does not necessarily

---

[114] Cal. Civ. Code § 1798.130(a)(5)(B) and (C).

[115] Cal. Civ. Code § 1798.130(a)(5).

need to be published in the policy itself, but organizations are variously required to disclose this information as part of other statutory provisions. As a result, organizations may prefer to pre-emptively disclose some additional pieces of information within their privacy policy or processing notice, rather than having to give this information out in response to each individual consumer request.

Data privacy policies or data processing notices should explain the following:

The categories of sources from which personal information is collected.[116]

This is an explanation of how the organization got hold of the consumer's personal information, if that information is not being collected directly. For example, some organizations may only act as service providers, in which case it would be beneficial to explain which organization in the data supply chain actually acted as the "business" that originally collected the data (and thus, the organization that is ultimately responsible for responding to consumers). In some industries, it is also common for organizations to share or purchase information, such as mailing lists or other contact details.

---

[116] Cal. Civ. Code § 1798.110(a)(2).

The categories of third parties with whom the business shares personal information.[117]

Along with an understanding of what the organization at issue does with personal information, consumers should also be able to easily understand where the data came from (see above), and where else it might go. Transparency is a key theme underlying many international data protection and privacy regimes, so it is only natural to see that same element enshrined in the CCPA. Rather than responding to individual customer requests on this topic, it is likely easier for an organization to explain the nature of its third-party data processors (service providers) at the outset of data collection. This can help minimize the burden associated with verifiable consumer requests.

The business or commercial purpose for collecting or selling personal information.[118]

Again, transparency is key. If consumers' personal information will be shared outside the organization, they should know why that information is being shared. Organizations often indicate the nature of the function using the information at issue. For example, contact details may be used for outreach and engagement, commercial information may be used for sales and marketing, network activity information may be used as a part of service provision or for license compliance, additional identifiers may be used for verification, etc.

---

[117] Cal. Civ. Code § 1798.110(a)(4).

[118] Cal. Civ. Code § 1798.110(a)(3).

As may become clear, there are similar but separate requirements that apply to organizations that sell personal information, as opposed to those that merely collect information. Section 135 deals with the notice and disclosure requirements that apply to these types of organizations. In addition to the above, organizations that sell consumer personal information to third parties will need to concern themselves with the "right to opt-out."

Right to opt-out

This is the right to request that a business that sells personal information to third parties no longer sell the consumer's personal information.[119]

Organizations engaged in selling consumer personal information will face compliance challenges slightly different from those organizations that merely collect and process personal information for their own use. Disclosure requirements for these organizations can be found in section 115 of the CCPA, although they substantially mirror the disclosure requirements outlined previously (i.e. full transparency around the data lifecycle). In addition, these organizations will need to comply with the "right to opt-out" found in section 120, which in turn dictates what must be included in the public privacy policy per section 135.

To start, consumers have the right to direct a business that sells their personal information to stop selling this

---

[119] Cal. Civ. Code § 1798.120.

information at any time.[120] This is the "right to opt-out." Businesses that sell personal information to third parties are required to notify consumers that their information may be sold, and that they have a right to opt-out of this sale.[121]

Before moving forward, organizations need to pause to consider what happens if a consumer does opt-out:

1. Can the technology at issue actually be manipulated to pause or stop the onward sale of the information?
2. Are there any primary or secondary business processes that would be impacted by this interruption?

Organizations are often structured around efficient hand-offs between one group and the next. Are these groups so tightly controlled that a consumer request can be effectively handled by one unit? Or does responsibility need to be allocated among the different groups involved:

- Those who are accountable for responding to opt-out requests;
- Those who need to be consulted or contacted; and
- Third parties that may also rely on this data?

How will that sale be affected? It is often useful to consider the full lifecycle of the personal information at issue, from data collection to storage to disposal, in order to understand all of the touchpoints inside and outside the organization.

Once this is complete, attention and energy can then be turned to developing supplemental processes that do not rely

---

[120] CCPA § 1798.120(a).

[121] CCPA § 1798.120(b).

on the data sale. Remember, an organization that sells personal information not only needs to manage consumer requests to opt-out as a process itself (i.e. outreach mechanism, responding within the proper time frame, documenting responses for compliance audit, passing on those requests internally to other functions, etc.), but also the effects of the process. How will the organization respond when consumers stop granting permission for the onward sale of data? Can permission be granted based on a smaller scope of data sale? Are alternative arrangements in place should a consumer completely remove their permissions? In short, organizations that rely on the sale of consumer personal information may face an existential crisis if consumers stop supporting their data processing activities.

Unlike the GDPR, consumers do not need to actively opt in to data-selling arrangements under the CCPA, and organizations may be able to continue dealing in personal data without the consent of the consumer. However, smart organizations will prepare for eventualities that do not involve data sale, assuming that at least some consumers will permanently exercise their right to opt-out when the statute takes effect. This may present daunting, long-term structural challenges for organizations that rely heavily on data sales revenue. Procedurally though, the remainder of the CCPA is relatively straightforward on what is required in terms of notice and disclosure.

Of course, any organization that sells personal information to third parties must disclose to consumers that the information may be sold, and that they have a right to opt-out of this sale. Section 135 goes on to require that this disclosure be provided via "a clear and conspicuous link on the business's Internet homepage, titled 'Do Not Sell My

Personal Information.'"[122] Consumers should be able to use this page to directly opt-out of the sale of their personal information, on top of the email or telephone outreach mechanism generally available. Organizations must also include a description of the right to opt-out along with a separate link to this page in any online privacy policies.[123] So, what does this look like in practice?

Much like the disclosure requirements explained above, organizations that sell personal information should consider a holistic approach to compliance. Rather than maintaining several different links on a web page (each possibly with its own process), a single privacy policy that outlines the right to opt-out in detail may be preferable. That master policy can pay a great deal of attention to the mechanisms that enable customers to exercise this right. For example, some organizations may be able to offer self-service tools that allow consumers to opt-out at their leisure – although note that organizations cannot compel consumers to create an account purely for the purposes of exercising this right (the issue then being whether the organization can actually function based on the unpredictable whims of consumers opting into and out of the sale of their information). Other organizations may maintain a separate opt-out process, or treat this request no different from any other verifiable consumer request that comes in via email or telephone.

Regardless of the actual way consumers can opt-out, the idea is that all detail relevant to this right lives in the same master policy document, thereby streamlining the management and

[122] CCPA § 1798.135(a)(1).

[123] CCPA § 1798.135(a)(2)(A), (B).

review of the policy and its related sub-processes. Organizations could put clear and conspicuous links across their web presence that read "Do Not Sell My Personal Information," and use this link to direct the consumer to the privacy policy (perhaps linking directly to the section of the policy at issue), rather than creating a separate web page. The goal is to minimize the amount of tangential processes that need ongoing maintenance and review. Ideally, everything related to privacy should be linked together.

Once a consumer opt-outs of the onward sale of their information, the organization must actually refrain from selling the information for at least 12 months.[124] After 12 months, the organization can reach out to the consumer to request permission to sell the personal information again.[125]

Right to deletion

This is the right to request that a business delete any personal information about the consumer that the business collected.[126]

Nowhere does the issue of inner workings become clearer than with regards to the right to deletion. Section 105 of the CCPA broadly states, "A consumer shall have the right to request that a business delete any personal information about the consumer which the business has collected from the

---

[124] CCPA § 1798.135(a)(4).

[125] CCPA § 1798.135(a)(5).

[126] Cal. Civ. Code § 1798.105.

consumer."[127] Businesses collecting personal information must, of course, disclose this right to deletion, and thus the privacy policy may be an ideal place to disclose all consumer privacy rights generally. This way, all privacy rights are consistently explained to all consumers, regardless of whether the right actually applies to the data at issue – something that can be analyzed, and explained, via the consumer response process.

The right to deletion is not absolute – the organization can continue to hold a consumer's personal information if it is necessary for a number of purposes. The CCPA recognizes there may be situations where organizations cannot realistically delete data.

Neither a business nor a service provider needs to comply with a request for deletion if the information is needed to: *128*

Complete a transaction, provide a good or service, or otherwise perform a contract "between the business and the consumer."[129]

This applies where the information to be deleted is necessary to complete the original transaction. For example, a customer's contact details are likely needed to provide a product or service, and cannot be realistically deleted mid-transaction. How would the customer actually receive what they paid for? In contrast, many organizations use their

---

[127] CCPA § 1798.105(a).

[128] Cal. Civ. Code § 1798.105(d)(1)–(9).

[129] Cal. Civ. Code § 1798.105(d)(1).

existing sales funnels as a marketing or reselling channel. If an organization is currently using information in furtherance of product or process *A*, and the customer has requested deletion with regards to product or process *B*, the organization needs to be able to segregate the information to comply with the consumer's request. This will help ensure that a single request for deletion does not inadvertently cause the deletion of all personal information related to that consumer. If the consumer still requests for the information to be deleted at the end of the transaction, that request should be honored (as there is no articulated business purpose for keeping or using the data anymore).

Detect security incidents or protect against malicious, deceptive, fraudulent, or illegal activity.[130]

This is especially relevant in the context of electronic information and logs. Good cybersecurity inherently requires accurate system logs to determine who accessed what system, when. Often this information cannot or should not be deleted. Some organizations may also track IP addresses or device IDs to help manage licenses for software and SaaS offerings. This information does not need to be deleted simply because a consumer requests deletion. However, the organization will need to understand precisely which data elements are used for which business purpose (e.g. completing a transaction versus security management). This will make it clearer to personnel why certain information is needed (and, consequently, how it is intended to be used at the organization). By making this information clear, those responsible for responding to consumer requests for deletion

---

[130] Cal. Civ. Code § 1798.105(d)(2).

can more quickly and easily identify which information is suitable for deletion, and which cannot (or should not) be deleted.

Note that this exception also includes language related to prosecution of offenses; it is not just about detecting incidents and protecting the organization, but also after-the-fact investigation and prosecution of those responsible.[131]

"Debug to identify and repair errors that impair existing intended functionality."[132]

This exception only applies to debugging efforts used in the identification and repair of existing functionality. This does not carve out a broad exception for organizations to hold personal information for future research and development projects; it only applies to active issues.

Exercise free speech.[133]

This exception allows an organization to hold consumer personal information for the purposes of exercising free speech, or another right provided by law. Presumably this is focused on the rights of the organization, as it may be hard to imagine a scenario where a consumer requests the deletion of their information, and in turn the organization replies that the information cannot be deleted because the information helps the consumer exercise their own rights (presumably, if a consumer was using personal information to exercise their

---

[131] Cal. Civ. Code § 1798.105(d)(2).

[132] Cal. Civ. Code § 1798.105(d)(3).

[133] Cal. Civ. Code § 1798.105(d)(4).

free speech, they would not request that the information be deleted, as they would no longer be exercising their right). It also specifies ensuring the right of another consumer to exercise their right of free speech.

This may be particularly relevant for news organizations, media outlets, and social media companies. Keep in mind that the definition of personal information under the CCPA includes broad language: "information that identifies, relates to, describes, is capable of being associated with, or could reasonably be linked, directly or indirectly, with a particular consumer or household." As a result, comments posted on a news board or web forum could be considered personal information (personal information includes information regarding a consumer's interaction with an Internet website – see § 1798.140(o)(1)(F)). For example, if someone posts a comment about the Governor of California on the webpage of a news article, that comment would theoretically contain the Governor's personal information. If the Governor attempted to exercise a right to delete that information, the news outlet could perhaps claim a free speech exemption. Organizations engaged in those industries should review relevant bodies of law related to constitutional guarantees of free speech in order to more clearly define what constitutes "exercising" this right though.

Engage in scientific, historical, or statistical research in the public interest.[134]

This exception comes with a few caveats. First, the research conducted must be "in the public interest." That is, an organization cannot use this exception as an excuse to hold consumer personal information for some nebulously defined research project. The research must actually be academic, subject to "public or peer-review."[135] In fact, the definition of "research" found in section 140 states that it "shall not be used for a commercial purpose."[136] The research must also adhere to all other applicable ethics and privacy laws (e.g. HIPAA for research involving personal health information).

Importantly, the research exception only applies if deleting the information at issue would impair the research. That is, if the scientific, historical, or statistical research can continue unimpacted by the loss of consumer personal information, it can (and should) be deleted upon request. Personal information could also be deidentified, so that the raw research data is still useful while preserving consumers' privacy. As a result, organizations looking to avail themselves of this exception will need to prepare for rebuttals to possible claims that the information can be deleted with minimal impact. Should an organization argue that it must retain consumer personal information for

---

[134] Cal. Civ. Code § 1798.105(d)(6).

[135] Ibid.

[136] Cal. Civ. Code § 1798.140(s)(9).

research purposes, it should be prepared to show how that personal information is vital to the research.

Finally, this exception only applies if the consumer has provided consent.[137] Therefore, in order to reject a request for deletion because the organization needs the information for research, the organization will likely need to demonstrate that the information is vital for research to continue, and that the consumer understands and consents. In effect, the consumer is basically consenting for their personal information to continue to be used – otherwise, without consent, it is unlikely the organization can continue using the information.

Comply with a legal obligation.[138]

This relates to a true legal obligation, not some policy, code of conduct, or industry standard. Should an organization wish to avail itself of this exception, it should be able to point to a specific statute, law, or official document (e.g. warrant, subpoena, etc.) that outlines the requirements relating to personal information.

That said, there are many scenarios in which data must be retained for legal reasons. Tax laws often require certain information to be saved for a period of time; contracts may also contain specific stipulations regarding data retention. Ideally, organizations should maintain a list or register of all

---

[137] Cal. Civ. Code § 1798.105(d)(6).

[138] Cal. Civ. Code § 1798.105(d)(8).

their legal obligations, as it can be useful to understand and analyze their evolving impact on the organization as a whole.

To "enable solely internal uses that are reasonably aligned with the expectations of the consumer based on the consumer's relationship with the business."[139]

This is an exception that allows for internal operations. Under the exception outlined here, it should not be an issue to share consumer information within the same silo, product, or business area, as long as those internal uses are "reasonably aligned with the expectations of the consumer."

For example, many organizations rely on existing customers for potential upsell or resell revenue. Most customers will likely expect a bit of material to be sent their way with regards to existing products or services (e.g. software updates, hardware upgrades). It should also be reasonable for them to expect their personal information to be used in furtherance of the overall business relationship – account management, invoicing, technical support, etc.

It may be unreasonable to reach across silos or areas and share information. Consumers who purchase laptops expect to hear more about laptops – they likely do not expect or want to hear more about other devices (if they did, they would have indicated this). Again, it is crucial to understand what data is being used for exactly what purpose. Data processing activities need to be kept separate – ideally, each data element or information identifier is being used for one business purpose at a time. That way, functions across the organization can be clear on why the information is in use

---

[139] Cal. Civ. Code § 1798.105(d)(7).

for each individual process, which in turn helps provide clarity on what data can be deleted (and who is responsible for that).

To "otherwise use the consumer's personal information, internally, in a lawful manner that is compatible with the context in which the consumer provided the information."[140]

Again, this carves out an exception for internal processing performed in furtherance of the original, overall objective.

Any organization that receives a valid request for deletion must delete the consumer's personal information.[141] This may seem obvious on its face, but the key is in actually demonstrating compliance. How can an organization prove it has deleted personal information if the personal information no longer exists? Organizations need to therefore consider the various documentation requirements associated with verifiable consumer requests, to help demonstrate that the actions taken by the organization actually did occur, and they did so in accordance with the law and within the right time frame. In this case, records of deletion could be maintained. Not an actual record of the information at issue, but rather, a record of what was deleted (e.g. "[Consumer name]'s contact details were deleted on XXX date in response to consumer request received on YYY date."). Ideally, this is all tied to the consumer response process, as it is likely that many different types of consumer requests will come through that channel. Track them all and

---

[140] Cal. Civ. Code § 1798.105(d)(9).

[141] CCPA § 1798.105(c).

document them appropriately. However, each issue will need to be dealt with individually based on the consumer and the information at issue.

Another procedural hurdle for organizations to consider comes with the onward notice of a deletion request. Organizations will need to direct any associated service providers to also delete the requested information from their records.[142] Consequently, organizations need to prepare notification mechanisms along the data supply chain as it relates to consumer information, along with associated contractual requirements that will flow out to service providers. Once a request is received and verified by the business, internal mechanisms should kick-off a notification process that advises associated service providers of the verified request (for their own compliance documentation) and the information requested to be deleted.

In turn, the service provider should notify the business that the request has been filled, either in writing or through some other certification process that indicates the deletion request was honored. Organizations may wish to impose time limits on when a service provider must respond to and/or honor a deletion request, so that the service provider's actions do not pose a liability to the business (for example, what if a business honors a consumer's request for deletion but the service provider does not? Who is at fault for the continued use of the information? Can the original organization prove it provided instructions for deletion to the service provider? Can the service provider prove the request was honored?). Much of compliance comes down to following documented

---

[142] CCPA § 1798.105(c).

processes and keeping records that demonstrate this – it is not just about following the law, but following the law in such a way that proves the organization continually manages its operations according to compliant practices.

There are, of course, technical considerations. First, can this actually be done? Can consumer information actually be deleted? Discussions with IT, systems engineers, database managers, and software developers will likely be key at this stage. Some tools and systems either cannot, or may not have been configured, to cleanly delete data on a point-by-point basis.

If deletion is not technically possible, are other deidentification methods available? Remember, the CCPA does not restrict the collection, use, retention, storage, or disclosure of consumer information that is either deidentified or in the aggregate,[143] so there may be workarounds if the information cannot be deleted but can otherwise be completely stripped of its identifying characteristics. This might include, for instance, certain types of encryption, especially if it can be made irreversible (such as by deleting or destroying the encryption key).

Organizations cannot discriminate against a consumer simply because the consumer exercised their rights under the CCPA.[144] For example, an organization cannot deny goods or services, or offer a different quality of goods or services, in an attempt to discourage consumers from exercising their

---

[143] Cal. Civ. Code § 1798.145(a)(5).

[144] Cal. Civ. Code § 1798.125(a).

rights.[145] However, an organization can charge different prices or provide different services to a consumer who has exercised their rights, as long as that difference is "reasonably related to the value provided to the consumer by the consumer's data."[146] In addition, organizations may offer financial incentives as compensation "for the collection of personal information, the sale of personal information, or the deletion of personal information" (although the consumer must give opt-in consent, which must be revocable at any time).[147]

Summary

Organizations must prepare a variety of internal and external-facing processes to ensure they comply with their new obligations. Covered entities need to consider a method that allows consumers to submit requests for information or deletion (including, at a minimum, a toll-free phone number, and if the business maintains a website, a web address).[148] Responses to such requests (called "data subject access requests," or "DSARs" in the EU) must be delivered free of charge within 45 days.[149] Much like the GDPR, that time period can be extended under certain circumstances,

---

[145] Cal. Civ. Code § 1798.125(a)(1)(A),(C).

[146] Cal. Civ. Code § 1798.125(a)(2).

[147] Cal. Civ. Code § 1798.125(b).

[148] CCPA § 1798.130(a)(1).

[149] CCPA § 1798.130(a)(2).

provided the organization gives notice to the consumer.[150] Additionally, "disclosures must be made in a readily useable format that allows the consumer to transmit this information from one entity to another entity without hindrance."[151] All of these things will require an innate understanding of the organization and its data processing activities in order to provide transparency into those activities (i.e. notice and disclosure). Furthermore, organizations must simultaneously prepare for the procedural impact of these new consumer rights, not only in terms of actually managing and replying to consumer requests, but also in the related internal inner workings.

As an organization tackles the procedural hurdles associated with consumer notice, disclosure, opt-out, and deletion requests, it will need to consider the substantive hurdles as well. As discussed earlier, what happens if a consumer requests that their information is no longer sold? How does that actually impact a business that relies on data sales for revenue? Similarly, what happens if a consumer requests that their information be deleted?

The clearest solution is to establish clear, public-facing information about processing and consumers' rights, and to link this to simple methods for exercising those rights. The organization can then digest requests so that they can be directed to the correct parts of the business, each of which should have clear processes for complying with requests,

---

[150] CCPA § 1798.130(a)(2).

[151] Ibid.

which can then be compiled centrally and any necessary responses can be directed to the consumer.

CHAPTER 6: SECURITY REQUIREMENTS

There are no prescriptive security requirements outlined in the CCPA. The only real place "security" is mentioned as a topic is in section 150. That section actually contains what is left of the original ballot proposal's private right of action, and it details how consumers can make a claim under the CCPA. In turn, some insight can be gained into the obligations of organizations, and how they can rebut consumer claims.

At the time of writing, consumers will only be able to institute a civil action against an organization for failure to secure data. Such a claim actually has several requirements under section 150. First, the personal information must be "nonencrypted or nonredacted."[152] So, an easy way for organizations to avoid liability under this section – and thus, perhaps a security suggestion, if not an outright requirement – is to simply encrypt all consumer personal information.

Note though, that "nonencrypted or nonredacted personal information" are defined in this section by virtue of reference to subparagraph (A) of paragraph (1) of subdivision (d) of section 1798.81.5 of the California Civil Code, which technically does not live in the CCPA itself. Somewhat curiously then, the legislative drafters of the CCPA have chosen to redefine "personal information" for their own purposes. Again, great care must be taken when reading parts

---

[152] Cal. Civ. Code § 1798.150(a)(1).

of a statute in order to understand how all of the parts fit together.

"Personal information," for purposes of a consumer civil suit under section 150, must then meet the definition outlined in section 81.5. There, "personal information" means either of the following:[153]

(1)

    (A) An individual's first name or first initial and his or her last name in combination with any one or more of the following data elements, when either the name or the data elements are not encrypted or redacted:

        (i)   Social Security number.

        (ii) Driver's license number or California identification card number.

        (iii) Account number, credit or debit card number, in combination with any required security code, access code, or password that would permit access to an individual's financial account.

        (iv) Medical information.

        (v) Health insurance information.

    (B) A username or email address in combination with a password or security question and answer that would permit access to an online account.

(2) "Medical information" means any individually identifiable information, in electronic or physical form,

---

[153] Cal. Civ. Code § 1798.81.5(d)(1)-(3).

regarding the individual's medical history or medical treatment or diagnosis by a health care professional.

(3) "Health insurance information" means an individual's insurance policy number or subscriber identification number, any unique identifier used by a health insurer to identify the individual, or any information in an individual's application and claims history, including any appeals records.

As can be seen, this definition of "personal information" is slightly more narrow than the definition provided in section 140 (almost anything that can directly or indirectly link, relate to, or be associated with a consumer). As a result, organizations should take special care to safeguard this information, in particular – Social Security numbers, identification card numbers, account numbers and payment information, medical information, and health insurance information – likely by means of encryption, or redaction where possible.

So, as it relates to security requirements under the CCPA – organizations have a "duty to implement and maintain reasonable security procedures and practices appropriate to the nature of the information."[154] Generally speaking, the security obligations imposed on organizations by the CCPA are really about maintaining "reasonable security." The idea is that applied security controls may differ depending on the organization and the data at issue. It is unlikely that all data will be treated the same for security purposes, so the law is specifically written to provide only a duty of maintaining

---

[154] Cal. Civ. Code § 1798.150(a)(1).

"reasonable security." What is considered "reasonable" is then left to the organization.

Any organization in the midst of a data governance project should truly consider a risk-based approach to project initiation, program development, and ongoing maintenance. This approach balances the risks to the information, the organization, and the consumer against the practicalities of securing the information. This allows the organization to define what it considers "reasonable security," which it can amend in later reviews if it finds that security measures are ineffective or impractical, or that security is excessively strict. Through an ongoing process of review and correction, the organization can develop a streamlined, effective, and "reasonable" set of security measures.

Different security controls are applied to different systems and databases – there likely is not a one-size-fits-all approach. Unfortunately, tailored-made systems are difficult to assess for liability purposes. If an issue were to arise, litigation may inevitably devolve into a battle of the experts, whereby one IT guru argues that the security is reasonable, while another IT guru argues that the security was not reasonable at all. Essentially, it becomes difficult to pin down what was reasonable in the circumstances at issue unless there is a systematic model for compliance based on objective risk analysis. Otherwise, the organization will be left arguing (at considerable cost) why their approach was reasonable in that particular instance.

A risk-based approach to IT security management lets the organization rely on its compliance program – a combination of people, process, and technology-driven solutions – to provide a model for consistent approaches to risk analysis and remediation. The organization ideally will not have to argue why its approach was reasonable in any given instance. Rather, it can argue that its program delivers a model for compliance based on risk. The idea is no different from grade school math – there is value in showing how one arrived at the answer, in addition to the answer itself.

Processes are often easier to analyze for compliance purposes than ad hoc activities because they exist as semi-stable templates. This is the benefit of risk management or risk control frameworks such as ISO 27001. Regardless of the facts and circumstances at play, the process outlines decision-making criteria and responses that apply in all scenarios. Ad hoc approaches to compliance, on the other hand, require a great level of understanding of the facts and circumstances at play in each individual case.

So, although the CCPA only imposes an obligation of "reasonable security," it is not difficult to see how this obligation actually works in practice. Good, "reasonable" security will likely involve a level of encryption surrounding the data elements outlined in section 81.5. It will also involve a risk-based approach to security management. Applying encryption more widely may also prove beneficial, because the loss of encrypted information poses no problem under the CCPA.

Section 150 includes some extra considerations. Subparagraph (a)(1) states that a consumer's right to pursue civil action applies when personal information "is subject to an unauthorized access and exfiltration, theft, or disclosure." It is important to consider the full range of data-loss scenarios, as each may pose liability to the organization. Data may be stolen, as is often the case with hackers. Data can also be stolen internally – either directly, through employees and personnel (e.g. someone looking to take work product, trade secrets, or client account information to their next employer); or indirectly, through consultants and contracts (e.g. Target's 2014 hack was caused in part by vulnerabilities with the heating, ventilation, and air conditioning provider). Data can also be inadvertently exposed – sending emails to the wrong person, or accidentally posting files on a public web page. There is no shortage of examples in the media that detail the latest embarrassing data breach. Many of these types of incidents can be controlled and contained through technological solutions (e.g. data loss prevention (DLP) tools). A level of general assurance can also be provided through internal training. Everyone at the organization should be aware of their responsibility for cybersecurity, data privacy, and good data governance. Make sure they understand how their actions, no matter how inadvertent or minor, can subject the whole organization to risk.

Remember that the CCPA really only requires organizations to maintain reasonable security. Ideally, this involves a risk-based approach to information security management and some element of training to ensure all personnel are aware of threats, liabilities, and how to avoid them.

CHAPTER 7: PENALTIES

Interestingly, the consumer enforcement mechanism outlined in section 150 is quite narrow in scope. In particular, consumer enforcement under the CCPA is much narrower than the provisions originally included in Mactaggart's ballot proposal. As mentioned earlier, consumers can only bring a civil action for failure to "implement and maintain reasonable security procedures and practices."[155] Consumer civil suits cannot be based on violations of any other section of the statute.[156] Therefore, at the time of writing, consumers will not be able to bring claims against an organization for, say, failure to respond to a consumer request within the appropriate time frame, or failure to delete data. Consumers may institute civil action against an organization only for loss of nonencrypted or nonredacted information caused by a failure to maintain reasonable security.[157]

The penalties under this provision are relatively small, although they can stack up, especially in a class-action case. Damages are limited to actual damages caused by the data's loss, or statutory damages ranging from $100–750 per consumer, per incident.[158] When determining the amount of

---

[155] Cal. Civ. Code § 1798.150(a).

[156] Cal. Civ. Code § 1798.150(c).

[157] Cal. Civ. Code § 1798.150(a).

[158] Cal. Civ. Code § 1798.150(a)(1)(A).

statutory damages, courts will consider "any one or more of the relevant circumstances [...] including, but not limited to": [159]

- The nature and seriousness of the misconduct
- The number of violations
- The persistence of the misconduct
- The length of time over which the misconduct occurred
- The wilfulness of the defendant's misconduct; and
- The defendant's assets, liabilities, and net worth

Whichever amount is higher – statutory or actual – will be the amount used for damages. So, if a consumer cannot demonstrate actual financial harm caused by the data loss, they will be limited to the statutory cap. Of course, the court may also grant an injunction, or any other relief that it deems proper.[160]

It is quite complicated to enforce the consumer civil suit provision, however. When pursuing a case for statutory damages, a consumer must provide 30 days' written notice before initiating an action against an organization.[161] Note that this notice is not required to initiate an action solely for

---

[159] Cal. Civ. Code § 1798.150(a)(2).

[160] Cal. Civ. Code § 1798.150(a)(1)(B),(C).

[161] Cal. Civ. Code § 1798.150(b).

actual damages suffered; the 30-day notice rule only applies to cases pursuing statutory damages.[162]

In their notice, the consumer should identify specific provisions of the CCPA that are alleged to have been violated.[163] The organization then has 30 days to cure the violation. Assuming the violation is cured, the organization should provide a written statement to the consumer explaining that the violation has been resolved and that no further violations will occur. Under these conditions, no action for statutory damages may proceed.[164]

If an organization then continues to violate the CCPA "in breach of the express written statement provided to the consumer," only then can the consumer initiate an action against the organization.[165] Technically, this action is only to enforce the written statement, and to pursue statutory damages for each breach of the statement.[166]

Remember that consumers can only initiate action against an organization for failure to maintain reasonable security. Conversely, California's attorney general can bring a suit for violation of any part of the statute, e.g. failure to respond to a consumer request within 45 days. Here, penalties for

---

[162] Cal. Civ. Code § 1798.150(b).

[163] Ibid.

[164] Ibid.

[165] Ibid.

[166] Ibid.

statutory violations are limited to $2,500 per violation, up to $7,500 for each intentional violation.[167] Injunction is also available as a remedy.[168]

Interestingly, section 155(b) states that, "A business shall be in violation of this title if it fails to cure any alleged violation within 30 days after being notified of alleged noncompliance."[169] Perhaps, then, the attorney general will be responsible for notifying organizations of potential violations, in a manner similar to that prescribed for initiating consumer civil suits. However, at the time of writing, the procedural mechanisms are not entirely clear. Based on the current iteration of the CCPA, it seems likely that the attorney general will notify organizations of alleged noncompliance at least 30 days before bringing an action against them. That said, the law is still subject to legislative revision, so ideally this process will be outlined in more detail over time.

---

[167] Cal. Civ. Code § 1798.155(b).

[168] Ibid.

[169] Ibid.

CHAPTER 8: BREACH NOTIFICATIONS

California already has rules governing data breaches and breach notification in sections 80–84 of the California Civil Code,[170] which deal with the maintenance of "customer records."

Section 82(a) deals with data breach notifications for a business, and it covers several areas. First, there are requirements that apply to an organization that "owns or licenses computerized data that includes personal information." Any "person or business that conducts business in California" that owns or licenses such information is required to disclose a data security breach to California residents. Here, a "breach" is defined as the unauthorized acquisition of unencrypted personal information. A breach may also include the loss of encrypted information, if the respective encryption key or other security credential was also lost. The important point is whether the organization has "a reasonable belief that the encryption key or security credential could render that (encrypted) personal information readable or useable." Ultimately, the issue is whether the organization lost readily readable or useable information.

If an organization that owns or licenses personal information suffers a breach, it is required to disclose it following either discovery or notification of the breach. Disclosures are to be made to California residents "in the most expedient time possible and without unreasonable delay." What that time

---

[170] Cal. Civ. Code § 1798.82.

frame will actually look like in practice will likely be dictated by evolving case law, because what constitutes an "unreasonable delay" may be different depending on the circumstances of the case at issue. The law does point out that expediency may be dictated by "any measures necessary to determine the scope of the breach and restore the reasonable integrity of the data system." As a result, any forensic analysis, technical investigations, or remediation and clean-up activities may provide a justifiable, "reasonable" delay. However, that does not permit organizations to use these activities as excuses to avoid the inevitable. California residents need to be notified, and in deference to their privacy rights (as the organization lost their data), disclosure should be made as soon as realistically possible.

In practice, this means organizations need to develop an incident response management process that facilitates quick and efficient investigation of issues. Should a security event occur, the organization should be poised to not only respond to the incident itself, but also to analyze the privacy impact and, in turn, notify affected consumers. This requires a great deal of coordination among IT or information security functions, the general counsel or legal department, and any marketing or public relations personnel who can help craft the actual disclosure message. Technical employees are required to understand, investigate, and eliminate the breach (while also learning from the issue in order to avoid similar issues in the future); legal is necessary to determine the threshold analysis required for disclosure, and to prepare the organization for any potential litigation or liability; and marketing/PR is needed to help with outreach to customers, business partners, investors, and potentially media outlets, who all may be interested in what is going on.

Ideally, all personnel at an organization should have a general understanding of information security issues and the symptoms of a possible attack or event. This is why awareness training is critical for all staff – everyone in the organization plays a role in managing information security. Of course, certain personnel play much larger roles (e.g. IT/IS). Not all employees need to understand the incident response management process. For example, it is likely unnecessary for front-end sales staff to understand the internal investigation and escalation processes related to information security incidents. Most personnel just need to understand who to contact if they think there is an issue. Dedicated support staff can take it from there, engaging in the necessary investigation and analysis to determine whether the issue actually rises to the level of an information security event or full-blown data breach. Those staff can contact relevant parties (e.g. legal, PR, senior management, etc.) as necessary.

Slightly different rules apply to organizations that maintain personal information that the business does not own. Those organizations are required to notify the owner or licensee of such information "immediately following discovery."[171] There are no carve-outs for measures to restore the integrity of the system, or questions of what constitutes reasonable vs. unreasonable delay. The notification must be made immediately, as soon as the breach is discovered. This will require close coordination between relevant teams or personnel that manage the incident response process.

---

[171] Cal. Civ. Code § 1798.82(b).

The statute goes on to provide detail related to the actual form and substance of the notification itself. Subparagraph (d) of section 82 outlines certain requirements. The notification must be "written in plain language, [...] titled 'Notice of Data Breach.'" It must also include certain details related to the breach, formatted in certain ways.

At a minimum, the following detail must be included in the breach notification:[172]

- The date that the notice is provided
- The name and contact information of the reporting person or business
- A list of the types of personal information that were or are reasonably believed to have been the subject of a breach
- A general description of the breach incident, if that information is possible to determine at the time the notice is provided
- Any of the following, if it is possible to determine at the time the notice is provided:
  - The date of the breach
  - The estimated date of the breach
  - The date range within which the breach occurred
- Whether notification was delayed as a result of a law enforcement investigation
- The toll-free telephone numbers and addresses of major credit reporting agencies if the breach exposed Social

---

[172] Cal. Civ. Code § 1798.82(d)(2)(A)–(G).

Security numbers, driver's license numbers, or California identification card numbers
- An offer to provide "appropriate identity theft prevention and mitigation services" to affected individuals at no cost for at least 12 months. However, this only applies if:
  o The person or business providing the notification was the source of the breach
  o The breach exposed Social Security numbers, driver's license numbers, or California identification card numbers

This detail must be presented under the following headings:[173]

- "What Happened"
- "What Information Was Involved"
- "What We Are Doing"
- "What You Can Do"
- "For More Information"

There are even formatting requirements. Titles and headings "shall be clearly and conspicuously displayed," the notice must be designed "to call attention to the nature and significance of the information it contains," and the text can be no smaller than ten-point font.[174]

---

[173] Cal. Civ. Code § 1798.82(d)(1).

[174] Cal. Civ. Code § 1798.82(d)(1)(A)–(C).

All of the above apply to written notices, but written notices are not the only method available to organizations. Should an organization choose to use a written notice, the statute helpfully provides a model security breach notification form – see Table 2.

Table 2: Model Security Breach Notification Form

[NAME OF INSTITUTION / LOGO]   _____ _____
Date: [insert date]

NOTICE OF DATA BREACH

What Happened?

What Information Was Involved?	
What We Are Doing.	
What You Can Do.	
Other Important Information. [insert other important information]	
For More Information.	Call [telephone number] or go to [Internet Website]

Other methods of notice are available, though. If the organization can demonstrate that the cost of providing individual notices would exceed $250,000, the number of affected people exceeds 500,000, or sufficient contact information is not available, the organization can rely on "substitute notice."[175] Substitute notice requires all of the following:[176]

- Email notice when the organization has an email address for those affected
- If the organization maintains a web page, there should be "conspicuous posting" of the notice there for at least 30 days.

  "conspicuous posting [...] means providing a link to the notice on the home page or first significant page after entering the Internet Web site that is in larger type than the surrounding text, or in contrasting type, font, or color to the surrounding text of the same size, or set off from the surrounding text of the same size by symbols or other marks that call attention to the link"

- Notification to major state-wide media

In the event of a security breach involving only login credentials (i.e. a username or email address, in combination with a password or security question and answer that would permit access to an online account), the organization may provide notice by directing affected individuals to promptly change their password and related security questions or answers, or to take other appropriate steps to protect any

---

[175] Cal. Civ. Code § 1798.82(j)(3).

[176] Cal. Civ. Code § 1798.82(j)(3)(A)–(C).

online accounts that use the same login credentials.[177] It should be noted that if the breach involves login credentials for an email account provided by the organization, sending a notification to that affected email address does not constitute notice.[178] In such cases, the organization should rely on one of the other notice methods mentioned above (e.g. conspicuous posting on the organization's website).

It is important to note that penalties for violations of those sections of the California Civil Code dealing with the maintenance of "customer records" are separate from the penalties outlined in the CCPA.[179] Any customer may initiate civil action to recover damages caused by violation of this statute.[180] Additional penalties apply to organizations that violate section 1798.83 of the statute, which deals with organizations that share personal information with third parties, knowing those third parties intend to use the information for direct marketing purposes. This is explained in Chapter 9.

---

[177] Cal. Civ. Code § 1798.82(j)(4).

[178] Cal. Civ. Code § 1798.82(j)(5).

[179] Cal. Civ. Code § 1798.84.

[180] Cal. Civ. Code § 1798.84(b).

CHAPTER 9: OTHER RELATED LAWS – MAINTAINING CUSTOMER RECORDS

There are rules in California statute that govern the maintenance and disposal of customer records. Although the overlap with those laws is somewhat confusing, they should be noted as they cover many of the same or similar topics.

For example, there are rules that apply to third parties that use personal information for direct marketing, and they are substantially similar to the "right of access" rules. Here, the rules apply to:

- A "business" which has "an established business relationship with a customer"; and ...
- The business disclosed personal information to third parties within the preceding calendar year; and ...
- "the business knows or reasonably should know that the third parties used the personal information for the third parties' direct marketing purposes"

If these apply, then the business must disclose certain information to customers that request this information.[181] It is important to note that these obligations do not apply to "a business with fewer than 20 full-time or part-time employees."[182]

---

[181] Cal. Civ. Code § 1798.83(a).

[182] Cal. Civ. Code § 1798.83(c)(1).

Note, the language here uses "customer" rather than "consumer," which is used in the CCPA. "Customer" is defined as "an individual who provides personal information to a business for the purpose of purchasing or leasing a product or obtaining a service from the business."[183] So, under this provision, a business needs to prepare responses to all customers, not just California residents (i.e. "consumers").

There is a specific definition of "personal information" used with regards to this provision. That is, section 1798.83 does not reference the definition of "personal information" found in relevant portions of the CCPA dealing with "right of access" requests. As a result, organizations that collect personal information will be required to disclose certain things; organizations that sell personal information will be required to disclose certain things; and, organizations that give personal information to third parties who in turn use it for marketing will be required to disclose certain things. This may seem like a compliance challenge, but the solution is actually quite simple, transparency. The more an organization can provide insight into its data processing activities in full detail, the less likely that organization will get tripped up by the various reporting requirements found in California law, and other national and international laws.

For purposes of disclosure under section 1798.83, "personal information" is defined as all of the following categories:[184]

- Name and address

---

[183] Cal. Civ. Code § 1798.80(c).

[184] Cal. Civ. Code § 1798.83(e)(6)(A).

- Electronic mail address
- Age or date of birth
- Names of children
- Electronic mail or other addresses of children
- Number of children
- The age or gender of children
- Height
- Weight
- Race
- Religion
- Occupation
- Telephone number
- Education
- Political party affiliation
- Medical condition
- Drugs, therapies, or medical products or equipment used
- The kind of product the customer purchased, leased, or rented
- Real property purchased, leased, or rented
- The kind of service provided
- Social Security number
- Bank account number
- Credit card number
- Debit card number
- Bank or investment account, debit card, or credit card balance
- Payment history

- Information pertaining to the customer's creditworthiness, assets, income, or liabilities

As can be seen, the categories of personal information provided in section 1798.83 are much more detailed than the categories of personal information provided in the CCPA.

So, if an organization provides personal information to third parties, and those third parties then use it for their own direct marketing purposes, the organization must disclose certain things about that arrangement to its customers. That process requires a few things.

First, information must be provided to customers free of charge.[185] This theme is increasingly common in data privacy laws. The idea is that companies cannot charge customers in an attempt to discourage transparency; people should be able to freely know how their data is used.

Second, the organization must designate either a mailing address, email address, telephone, or fax number where customer requests can be sent.[186] Once this is complete, the organization must then do at least one of the following:

- All agents, managers, and employees "who regularly have contact with customers" must be informed of the contact details so they can provide that information to customers.[187] Affected organizations will need to prepare relevant training materials, and document that

---

[185] Cal. Civ. Code § 1798.83(a).

[186] Cal. Civ. Code § 1798.83(b)(1).

[187] Cal. Civ. Code § 1798.83(b)(1)(A).

such training occurred, in order to effectively demonstrate that it met its obligations to instruct employees.

OR

- Contact details must be "readily available upon request of a customer at every place of business in California where the business or its agents regularly have contact with customers."[188] Ideally, this is already a natural occurrence – organizations should make it easy for consumers to contact them with questions regarding personal information, regardless of where the customer is located (one more reason to design a global, external privacy policy that is readily accessible across an organization's web presence).

OR

- Create web links to its privacy policies. Organizations can do so by either of the following:
  o Add to the home page of its Web site a link to a page titled "Your Privacy Rights"[189]

The first page of the resulting link must provide the contact details for submitting customer requests (i.e. mailing

---

[188] Cal. Civ. Code § 1798.83(b)(1)(C).

[189] Cal. Civ. Code § 1798.83(b)(1)(B).

address, email address, telephone or fax number).[190] It must also describe a customer's rights as they apply to this section of law (not the provisions of the CCPA).[191]

OR

- "Add the words 'Your Privacy Rights' to the home page's link to the business's privacy policy."[192]

In this case, the words "Your Privacy Rights," must be in the same style and size as the original link to the privacy policy.[193]

There are other requirements related to formatting the text of the words "Your Privacy Rights" for organizations that do not maintain a privacy policy. This is inadvisable, though. All organizations, regardless of how or where they operate, should prepare and publish a privacy policy or data processing notice. This is not only a sensible business strategy in today's economy, but also an explicit requirement of many other state and sector-specific privacy laws that likely also apply to the organization.

Regardless of how the customer makes their request, the organization must reply in either writing or email.[194] The

---

[190] Cal. Civ. Code § 1798.83(b)(1)(B).

[191] Ibid.

[192] Ibid.

[193] Ibid.

[194] Cal. Civ. Code § 1798.83(a)(1),(2).

response must include a listing of all of the categories outlined above that were disclosed "for the third parties' direct marketing purposes during the immediately preceding calendar year."[195] It must also include the names and addresses of all third parties that received personal information for their direct marketing purposes in the preceding calendar year.[196] However, organizations are only obligated to reply to a customer "once during the course of any calendar year."[197] In addition, organizations are not obligated "to provide information associated with specific individuals and may provide the information required by this section in standardized format."[198]

Responses must be provided within 30 days (not the 45 granted by the CCPA).[199] If the organization receives a request for information outside of one of its dedicated channels, the organization must provide a response "within a reasonable period […] but not to exceed 150 days from the date received."[200] Nevertheless, organizations would be well advised to align themselves against a single, limited time frame for responding to all consumer requests for information, rather than trying to manage requests separately

---

[195] Cal. Civ. Code § 1798.83(a)(1).

[196] Cal. Civ. Code § 1798.83(a)(2).

[197] Cal. Civ. Code § 1798.83(c)(1).

[198] Cal. Civ. Code § 1798.83(b)(3).

[199] Cal. Civ. Code § 1798.83(b)(1)(C).

[200] Ibid.

according to different communication channels, and thus different time frame requirements. It will likely be much easier to use one standard across the entire organization.

Part of the consumer response process should also involve follow-up communications, as consumers are likely to ask clarifying questions or request additional information. Personnel responsible for responding to consumers should be educated on proper response protocols. Communications should also be documented to track what was said and when. This is not only important in demonstrating compliance, but also in defending against legal claims. If an organization is alleged to have violated a provision of section 1798.83, it may be able to defend itself against those claims by providing evidence that it ultimately did respond to the consumer request properly, with complete and accurate information, within a certain time frame.[201]

Some organizations that share personal information with third parties for direct marketing purposes may already offer a way for their customers to either agree to, or opt-out of, such sharing. Keep in mind that under the CCPA, the right to opt-out only really applies to "a business that sells personal information […] to third parties," and not necessarily those organizations that merely disclose information to third parties.[202] However, if an organization does offer a way for customers to exercise choice around sharing data with third parties, the organization can comply

---

[201] Cal. Civ. Code § 1798.84(d).

[202] Cal. Civ. Code § 1798.120.

with the disclosure requirements set out in section 1798.83(a) by simply notifying the customer of their right to prevent disclosure, and providing a cost-free means to exercise that right.[203]

Failure to meet the disclosure requirements of section 1798.83 can subject a company to civil actions initiated by customers.[204] Civil penalties are currently limited to $500 per violation, or up to $3,000 for willful, reckless, or intentional violations.[205] These fines are cumulative, though, and can be imposed on an organization in addition to fines imposed for violations of CCPA statutes.[206] Prevailing plaintiffs are also entitled to recover "reasonable attorney's fees and costs," which can increase the ultimate cost of litigation for a liable organization.[207] It may also encourage a certain degree of vexatious litigation against organizations, in the hope that an organization will settle any claims before potentially proceeding to court (and in turn, increasing the amount of attorney's fees that the organization may have to pay for). As a result, organizations should take special care to comply with section 1798.83 disclosure requirements, in addition to the disclosure requirements in the CCPA.

---

[203] Cal. Civ. Code § 1798.83(c)(2).

[204] Cal. Civ. Code § 1798.84(b).

[205] Cal. Civ. Code § 1798.84(c).

[206] Cal. Civ. Code § 1798.84(h).

[207] Cal. Civ. Code § 1798.84(g).

California businesses are also required to take reasonable steps to dispose of customer records in a way that makes them unreadable or undecipherable.[208] In addition, businesses are required to "implement and maintain reasonable security procedures and practices appropriate to the nature of the information, to protect [it] from unauthorized access, destruction, use, modification, or disclosure," similar to Article 30 of the GDPR and various other US state data breach laws.[209]

---

[208] Cal. Civ. Code § 1798.81.

[209] Cal. Civ. Code § 1798.81.5(b),(c).

CHAPTER 10: FUTURE DEVELOPMENTS OF THE CCPA

One of the biggest challenges to complying with the CCPA is that the law is a continual work in progress. Provisions can be added, or language changed, based on legislative revisions that may continue up to the January 1, 2020, implementation date.

As of April 2019, seven public forums have been held throughout California to solicit public comments on the CCPA. Some changes to the CCPA have been proposed as a result of that process. For example, in late February 2019, California State Senator Hannah-Beth Jackson introduced legislation that would expand the private right of action. Senate Bill 561 would amend the language of CCPA section 1798.150 to allow "any consumer whose rights under this title are violated" to pursue civil action against an organization, not just those consumers "whose nonencrypted or nonredacted personal information [...] is subject to an unauthorized access."[210] This would allow consumers to pursue action for any statutory violation, even procedural violations such as failing to respond within the appropriate time frame. The bill would also remove the 30-day cure period afforded to organizations accused of a statutory violation (although remember that consumers can bring an

---

[210] SB-561 § 1798.150(a),(c).

action for actual, pecuniary damages at any time).[211]. As a result, consumers could theoretically bring an action for *any* statutory violation of the CCPA as soon as it occurs. SB-561 failed to pass the California Senate on May 16, 2019, but this does not prevent the introduction of its provisions (or others) by virtue of some other legislative amendment.[212]

There are many other proposed amendments:

- Assembly Bill 25, introduced in December 2018, would amend the definition of "consumer" found in section 1798.140(g) to exclude people whose personal information has been collected as part of the employment process (e.g. application, hiring, contracting, etc.).[213] If ratified, AB-25 would greatly reduce the administrative burden for organizations required to comply with the CCPA, as it would essentially remove HR-related processing from the scope of the law

- Assembly Bill 846 would amend section 1798.125(b) to allow organizations to offer other types of financial

---

[211] Cal. Civ. Code § 1798.150(b).

[212] *www.jdsupra.com/legalnews/ccpa-bill-to-expand-private-right-of-65974/*.

[213] AB-25 § 1798.140(g)(1),(2).

incentives, including gift cards or certificates, discounts, or loyalty/rewards programs[214]

- Assembly Bill 873 would slightly simplify the definition of "deidentified" data.[215] It would also remove "household" from the definition of "personal information"[216] (AB-1355 is similar)
- Assembly Bill 874 would explicitly clarify that "personal information" does not include deidentified or aggregate data[217]
- Assembly Bill 950 would require organizations to disclose the average monetary value of consumer personal information, and update this information on their privacy policy every 90 days[218]
- Assembly Bill 1202 would require data brokers to register with and disclose certain things to the attorney general's office[219]

---

[214] AB-846 § 1798.125(b)(1).

[215] AB-873 § 1798.140(h).

[216] AB-873 § 1798.140(o)(1).

[217] AB-874 § 1798.140(o)(3).

[218] AB-950 § 1798.91.01(a).

[219] AB-1202 § 1798.99.82.

- Assembly Bill 1281 would require California businesses using facial recognition technology to post "clear and conspicuous" physical signs at the entrance of every location to disclose the use of such technology[220]

Of course, there may be other amendments proposed as time goes on. The California attorney general's office also announced that it intends to release a Notice of Proposed Regulatory Action sometime in fall 2019, in conjunction with further potential opportunities for public comment, in an effort to facilitate continued revision of the law and its implementing regulations. These channels may provide more information about compliance as the CCPA evolves over time.[221]

That said, organizations should not wait to see what develops with regards to the CCPA. Many of the proposed amendments simply clarify language, and none remove the core privacy rights already iterated. Therefore, organizations would be well advised to begin their compliance program implementation and development around existing elements of the CCPA.

---

[220] AB-1281 § 1798.300(b).

[221] *https://oag.ca.gov/sites/all/files/agweb/pdfs/privacy/ccpa-public-forum-ppt.pdf*.

CHAPTER 11: THE CCPA

The text as of April, 2019[222]

CIVIL CODE - CIV

DIVISION 3. OBLIGATIONS [1427 - 3273] *(Heading of Division 3 amended by Stats. 1988, Ch. 160, Sec. 14.)*

PART 4. OBLIGATIONS ARISING FROM PARTICULAR TRANSACTIONS [1738 - 3273] *(Part 4 enacted 1872.)*

TITLE 1.81.5. California Consumer Privacy Act of 2018 [1798.100 - 1798.199] *(Title 1.81.5 added by Stats. 2018, Ch. 55, Sec. 3.)*

1798.100.

   (a) A consumer shall have the right to request that a business that collects a consumer's personal information disclose to that consumer the categories and specific pieces of personal information the business has collected.

   (b) A business that collects a consumer's personal information shall, at or before the point of collection, inform consumers as to the categories of personal information to be collected and the purposes for which the categories of personal information shall be used. A

---

[222] *https://leginfo.legislature.ca.gov/faces/codes_displayText.xhtml?division=3.&part=4.&lawCode=CIV&title=1.81.5.*

business shall not collect additional categories of personal information or use personal information collected for additional purposes without providing the consumer with notice consistent with this section.

(c) A business shall provide the information specified in subdivision (a) to a consumer only upon receipt of a verifiable consumer request.

(d) A business that receives a verifiable consumer request from a consumer to access personal information shall promptly take steps to disclose and deliver, free of charge to the consumer, the personal information required by this section. The information may be delivered by mail or electronically, and if provided electronically, the information shall be in a portable and, to the extent technically feasible, in a readily useable format that allows the consumer to transmit this information to another entity without hindrance. A business may provide personal information to a consumer at any time, but shall not be required to provide personal information to a consumer more than twice in a 12-month period.

(e) This section shall not require a business to retain any personal information collected for a single, one-time transaction, if such information is not sold or retained by the business or to reidentify or otherwise link information that is not maintained in a manner that would be considered personal information.

(Amended (as added by Stats. 2018, Ch. 55, Sec. 3) by Stats. 2018, Ch. 735, Sec. 1. (SB 1121) Effective September 23, 2018. Section operative January 1, 2020, pursuant to Section 1798.198.)

1798.105.

(a) A consumer shall have the right to request that a business delete any personal information about the consumer which the business has collected from the consumer.

(b) A business that collects personal information about consumers shall disclose, pursuant to Section 1798.130, the consumer's rights to request the deletion of the consumer's personal information.

(c) A business that receives a verifiable consumer request from a consumer to delete the consumer's personal information pursuant to subdivision (a) of this section shall delete the consumer's personal information from its records and direct any service providers to delete the consumer's personal information from their records.

(d) A business or a service provider shall not be required to comply with a consumer's request to delete the consumer's personal information if it is necessary for the business or service provider to maintain the consumer's personal information in order to:

   (1) Complete the transaction for which the personal information was collected, provide a good or service requested by the consumer, or reasonably anticipated within the context of a business's ongoing business relationship with the consumer, or otherwise perform a contract between the business and the consumer.

   (2) Detect security incidents, protect against malicious, deceptive, fraudulent, or illegal activity; or prosecute those responsible for that activity.

(3) Debug to identify and repair errors that impair existing intended functionality.

(4) Exercise free speech, ensure the right of another consumer to exercise his or her right of free speech, or exercise another right provided for by law.

(5) Comply with the California Electronic Communications Privacy Act pursuant to Chapter 3.6 (commencing with Section 1546) of Title 12 of Part 2 of the Penal Code.

(6) Engage in public or peer-reviewed scientific, historical, or statistical research in the public interest that adheres to all other applicable ethics and privacy laws, when the businesses' deletion of the information is likely to render impossible or seriously impair the achievement of such research, if the consumer has provided informed consent.

(7) To enable solely internal uses that are reasonably aligned with the expectations of the consumer based on the consumer's relationship with the business.

(8) Comply with a legal obligation.

(9) Otherwise use the consumer's personal information, internally, in a lawful manner that is compatible with the context in which the consumer provided the information.

(Amended (as added by Stats. 2018, Ch. 55, Sec. 3) by Stats. 2018, Ch. 735, Sec. 2. (SB 1121) Effective September 23, 2018. Section operative January 1, 2020, pursuant to Section 1798.198.)

1798.110.

(a) A consumer shall have the right to request that a business that collects personal information about the consumer disclose to the consumer the following:

  (1) The categories of personal information it has collected about that consumer.

  (2) The categories of sources from which the personal information is collected.

  (3) The business or commercial purpose for collecting or selling personal information.

  (4) The categories of third parties with whom the business shares personal information.

  (5) The specific pieces of personal information it has collected about that consumer.

(b) A business that collects personal information about a consumer shall disclose to the consumer, pursuant to paragraph (3) of subdivision (a) of Section 1798.130, the information specified in subdivision (a) upon receipt of a verifiable consumer request from the consumer.

(c) A business that collects personal information about consumers shall disclose, pursuant to subparagraph (B) of paragraph (5) of subdivision (a) of Section 1798.130:

  (1) The categories of personal information it has collected about that consumer.

  (2) The categories of sources from which the personal information is collected.

  (3) The business or commercial purpose for collecting or selling personal information.

(4) The categories of third parties with whom the business shares personal information.

(5) The specific pieces of personal information the business has collected about that consumer.

(d) This section does not require a business to do the following:

(1) Retain any personal information about a consumer collected for a single one-time transaction if, in the ordinary course of business, that information about the consumer is not retained.

(2) Reidentify or otherwise link any data that, in the ordinary course of business, is not maintained in a manner that would be considered personal information.

(Amended (as added by Stats. 2018, Ch. 55, Sec. 3) by Stats. 2018, Ch. 735, Sec. 3. (SB 1121) Effective September 23, 2018. Section operative January 1, 2020, pursuant to Section 1798.198.)

1798.115.

(a) A consumer shall have the right to request that a business that sells the consumer's personal information, or that discloses it for a business purpose, disclose to that consumer:

(1) The categories of personal information that the business collected about the consumer.

(2) The categories of personal information that the business sold about the consumer and the categories of third parties to whom the personal information was sold, by category or categories of personal

information for each third party to whom the personal information was sold.

(3) The categories of personal information that the business disclosed about the consumer for a business purpose.

(b) A business that sells personal information about a consumer, or that discloses a consumer's personal information for a business purpose, shall disclose, pursuant to paragraph (4) of subdivision (a) of Section 1798.130, the information specified in subdivision (a) to the consumer upon receipt of a verifiable consumer request from the consumer.

(c) A business that sells consumers' personal information, or that discloses consumers' personal information for a business purpose, shall disclose, pursuant to subparagraph (C) of paragraph (5) of subdivision (a) of Section 1798.130:

(1) The category or categories of consumers' personal information it has sold, or if the business has not sold consumers' personal information, it shall disclose that fact.

(2) The category or categories of consumers' personal information it has disclosed for a business purpose, or if the business has not disclosed the consumers' personal information for a business purpose, it shall disclose that fact.

(d) A third party shall not sell personal information about a consumer that has been sold to the third party by a business unless the consumer has received explicit notice and is provided an opportunity to exercise the right to opt-out pursuant to Section 1798.120.

(Amended (as added by Stats. 2018, Ch. 55, Sec. 3) by Stats. 2018, Ch. 735, Sec. 4. (SB 1121) Effective September 23, 2018. Section operative January 1, 2020, pursuant to Section 1798.198.)

1798.120.

(a) A consumer shall have the right, at any time, to direct a business that sells personal information about the consumer to third parties not to sell the consumer's personal information. This right may be referred to as the right to opt-out.

(b) A business that sells consumers' personal information to third parties shall provide notice to consumers, pursuant to subdivision (a) of Section 1798.135, that this information may be sold and that consumers have the "right to opt-out" of the sale of their personal information.

(c) Notwithstanding subdivision (a), a business shall not sell the personal information of consumers if the business has actual knowledge that the consumer is less than 16 years of age, unless the consumer, in the case of consumers between 13 and 16 years of age, or the consumer's parent or guardian, in the case of consumers who are less than 13 years of age, has affirmatively authorized the sale of the consumer's personal information. A business that willfully disregards the consumer's age shall be deemed to have had actual knowledge of the consumer's age. This right may be referred to as the "right to opt-in."

(d) A business that has received direction from a consumer not to sell the consumer's personal information or, in the case of a minor consumer's personal information has not received consent to sell the minor consumer's personal information shall be prohibited, pursuant to paragraph (4) of subdivision (a) of Section 1798.135, from selling the consumer's personal information after its receipt of the consumer's direction, unless the consumer subsequently provides express authorization for the sale of the consumer's personal information.

(Amended (as added by Stats. 2018, Ch. 55, Sec. 3) by Stats. 2018, Ch. 735, Sec. 5. (SB 1121) Effective September 23, 2018. Section operative January 1, 2020, pursuant to Section 1798.198.)

1798.125.

(a)

(1) A business shall not discriminate against a consumer because the consumer exercised any of the consumer's rights under this title, including, but not limited to, by:

(A) Denying goods or services to the consumer.

(B) Charging different prices or rates for goods or services, including through the use of discounts or other benefits or imposing penalties.

(C) Providing a different level or quality of goods or services to the consumer.

(D) Suggesting that the consumer will receive a different price or rate for goods or services or a different level or quality of goods or services.

(2) Nothing in this subdivision prohibits a business from charging a consumer a different price or rate, or from providing a different level or quality of goods or

services to the consumer, if that difference is reasonably related to the value provided to the consumer by the consumer's data.

(b)

(1) A business may offer financial incentives, including payments to consumers as compensation, for the collection of personal information, the sale of personal information, or the deletion of personal information. A business may also offer a different price, rate, level, or quality of goods or services to the consumer if that price or difference is directly related to the value provided to the consumer by the consumer's data.

(2) A business that offers any financial incentives pursuant to subdivision (a), shall notify consumers of the financial incentives pursuant to Section 1798.135.

(3) A business may enter a consumer into a financial incentive program only if the consumer gives the business prior opt-in consent pursuant to Section 1798.135 which clearly describes the material terms of the financial incentive program, and which may be revoked by the consumer at any time.

(4) A business shall not use financial incentive practices that are unjust, unreasonable, coercive, or usurious in nature.

(Amended (as added by Stats. 2018, Ch. 55, Sec. 3) by Stats. 2018, Ch. 735, Sec. 6. (SB 1121) Effective September 23, 2018. Section operative January 1, 2020, pursuant to Section 1798.198.)

1798.130.

(a) In order to comply with Sections 1798.100, 1798.105, 1798.110, 1798.115, and 1798.125, a business shall, in a form that is reasonably accessible to consumers:

(1) Make available to consumers two or more designated methods for submitting requests for information required to be disclosed pursuant to Sections 1798.110 and 1798.115, including, at a minimum, a toll-free telephone number, and if the business maintains an Internet Web site, a Web site address.

(2) Disclose and deliver the required information to a consumer free of charge within 45 days of receiving a verifiable consumer request from the consumer. The business shall promptly take steps to determine whether the request is a verifiable consumer request, but this shall not extend the business's duty to disclose and deliver the information within 45 days of receipt of the consumer's request. The time period to provide the required information may be extended once by an additional 45 days when reasonably necessary, provided the consumer is provided notice of the extension within the first 45-day period. The disclosure shall cover the 12-month period preceding the business's receipt of the verifiable consumer request and shall be made in writing and delivered through the consumer's account with the business, if the consumer maintains an account with the business, or by mail or electronically at the consumer's option if the consumer does not maintain an account with the business, in a readily useable format that allows the consumer to transmit this information from one entity

to another entity without hindrance. The business shall not require the consumer to create an account with the business in order to make a verifiable consumer request.

(3) For purposes of subdivision (b) of Section 1798.110:

(A) To identify the consumer, associate the information provided by the consumer in the verifiable consumer request to any personal information previously collected by the business about the consumer.

(B) Identify by category or categories the personal information collected about the consumer in the preceding 12 months by reference to the enumerated category or categories in subdivision (c) that most closely describes the personal information collected.

(4) For purposes of subdivision (b) of Section 1798.115:

(A) Identify the consumer and associate the information provided by the consumer in the verifiable consumer request to any personal information previously collected by the business about the consumer.

(B) Identify by category or categories the personal information of the consumer that the business sold in the preceding 12 months by reference to the enumerated category in subdivision (c) that most closely describes the personal information, and provide the categories of third parties to whom the consumer's personal information was sold in the preceding 12 months by reference to the enumerated category or categories in subdivision (c) that most closely describes the personal information sold. The business shall disclose the information in a list that is separate from a list generated for the purposes of subparagraph (C).

(C) Identify by category or categories the personal information of the consumer that the business disclosed for a business purpose in the preceding 12 months by reference to the enumerated category or categories in subdivision (c) that most closely describes the personal information, and provide the categories of third parties to whom the consumer's personal information was disclosed for a business purpose in the preceding 12 months by reference to the enumerated category or categories in subdivision (c) that most closely describes the personal information disclosed. The business shall disclose the information in a list that is separate from a list generated for the purposes of subparagraph (B).

(5) Disclose the following information in its online privacy policy or policies if the business has an online privacy policy or policies and in any California-specific description of consumers' privacy rights, or if the business does not maintain those policies, on its Internet Web site, and update that information at least once every 12 months:

(A) A description of a consumer's rights pursuant to Sections 1798.110, 1798.115, and 1798.125 and one or more designated methods for submitting requests.

(B) For purposes of subdivision (c) of Section 1798.110, a list of the categories of personal information it has collected about consumers in the preceding 12 months by reference to the enumerated category or categories in subdivision (c) that most closely describe the personal information collected.

(C) For purposes of paragraphs (1) and (2) of subdivision (c) of Section 1798.115, two separate lists:

(i) A list of the categories of personal information it has sold about consumers in the preceding 12 months by reference to the enumerated category or categories in subdivision (c) that most closely describe the personal information sold, or if the business has not sold consumers' personal information in the preceding 12 months, the business shall disclose that fact.

(ii) A list of the categories of personal information it has disclosed about consumers for a business purpose in the preceding 12 months by reference to the enumerated category in subdivision (c) that most closely describe the personal information disclosed, or if the business has not disclosed consumers' personal information for a business purpose in the preceding 12 months, the business shall disclose that fact.

(6) Ensure that all individuals responsible for handling consumer inquiries about the business's privacy

practices or the business's compliance with this title are informed of all requirements in Sections 1798.110, 1798.115, 1798.125, and this section, and how to direct consumers to exercise their rights under those sections.

(7) Use any personal information collected from the consumer in connection with the business's verification of the consumer's request solely for the purposes of verification.

(b) A business is not obligated to provide the information required by Sections 1798.110 and 1798.115 to the same consumer more than twice in a 12-month period.

(c) The categories of personal information required to be disclosed pursuant to Sections 1798.110 and 1798.115 shall follow the definition of personal information in Section 1798.140.

(Amended (as added by Stats. 2018, Ch. 55, Sec. 3) by Stats. 2018, Ch. 735, Sec. 7. (SB 1121) Effective September 23, 2018. Section operative January 1, 2020, pursuant to Section 1798.198.)

1798.135.

(a) A business that is required to comply with Section 1798.120 shall, in a form that is reasonably accessible to consumers:

(1) Provide a clear and conspicuous link on the business's Internet homepage, titled "Do Not Sell My Personal Information," to an Internet Web page that enables a consumer, or a person authorized by the consumer, to opt-out of the sale of the consumer's personal information. A business shall not require a

consumer to create an account in order to direct the business not to sell the consumer's personal information.

(2) Include a description of a consumer's rights pursuant to Section 1798.120, along with a separate link to the "Do Not Sell My Personal Information" Internet Web page in:

> (A) Its online privacy policy or policies if the business has an online privacy policy or policies.
>
> (B) Any California-specific description of consumers' privacy rights.

(3) Ensure that all individuals responsible for handling consumer inquiries about the business's privacy practices or the business's compliance with this title are informed of all requirements in Section 1798.120 and this section and how to direct consumers to exercise their rights under those sections.

(4) For consumers who exercise their right to opt-out of the sale of their personal information, refrain from selling personal information collected by the business about the consumer.

(5) For a consumer who has opted-out of the sale of the consumer's personal information, respect the consumer's decision to opt-out for at least 12 months before requesting that the consumer authorize the sale of the consumer's personal information.

(6) Use any personal information collected from the consumer in connection with the submission of the

consumer's opt-out request solely for the purposes of complying with the opt-out request.

(b) Nothing in this title shall be construed to require a business to comply with the title by including the required links and text on the homepage that the business makes available to the public generally, if the business maintains a separate and additional homepage that is dedicated to California consumers and that includes the required links and text, and the business takes reasonable steps to ensure that California consumers are directed to the homepage for California consumers and not the homepage made available to the public generally.

(c) A consumer may authorize another person solely to opt-out of the sale of the consumer's personal information on the consumer's behalf, and a business shall comply with an opt-out request received from a person authorized by the consumer to act on the consumer's behalf, pursuant to regulations adopted by the Attorney General.

(Amended (as added by Stats. 2018, Ch. 55, Sec. 3) by Stats. 2018, Ch. 735, Sec. 8. (SB 1121) Effective September 23, 2018. Section operative January 1, 2020, pursuant to Section 1798.198.)

1798.140.

For purposes of this title:

(a) "Aggregate consumer information" means information that relates to a group or category of consumers, from which individual consumer identities have been removed, that is not linked or reasonably linkable to any consumer or household, including via a device. "Aggregate consumer information" does not mean one or more individual consumer records that have been de-identified.

(b) "Biometric information" means an individual's physiological, biological or behavioral characteristics, including an individual's deoxyribonucleic acid (DNA), that can be used, singly or in combination with each other or with other identifying data, to establish individual identity. Biometric information includes, but is not limited to, imagery of the iris, retina, fingerprint, face, hand, palm, vein patterns, and voice recordings, from which an identifier template, such as a faceprint, a minutiae template, or a voiceprint, can be extracted, and keystroke patterns or rhythms, gait patterns or rhythms, and sleep, health, or exercise data that contain identifying information.

(c) "Business" means:

(1) A sole proprietorship, partnership, limited liability company, corporation, association, or other legal entity that is organized or operated for the profit or financial benefit of its shareholders or other owners, that collects consumers' personal information, or on the behalf of which such information is collected and that alone, or jointly with others, determines the purposes and means of the processing of consumers' personal information, that does business in the State of California, and that satisfies one or more of the following thresholds:

(A) Has annual gross revenues in excess of twenty-five million dollars ($25,000,000), as adjusted pursuant to paragraph (5) of subdivision (a) of Section 1798.185.

(B) Alone or in combination, annually buys, receives for the business's commercial purposes, sells, or shares for commercial purposes, alone or in combination, the personal information of 50,000 or more consumers, households, or devices.

(C) Derives 50 percent or more of its annual revenues from selling consumers' personal information.

(2) Any entity that controls or is controlled by a business, as defined in paragraph (1), and that shares common branding with the business. "Control" or "controlled" means ownership of, or the power to vote, more than 50 percent of the outstanding shares of any class of voting security of a business; control in any manner over the election of a majority of the directors, or of individuals exercising similar functions; or the power to exercise a controlling influence over the management of a company. "Common branding" means a shared name, servicemark, or trademark.

(d) "Business purpose" means the use of personal information for the business's or a service provider's operational purposes, or other notified purposes, provided that the use of personal information shall be reasonably necessary and proportionate to achieve the operational purpose for which the personal information was collected or processed or for another operational purpose that is compatible with the context in which the personal information was collected. Business purposes are:

(1) Auditing related to a current interaction with the consumer and concurrent transactions, including, but not limited to, counting ad impressions to unique visitors, verifying positioning and quality of ad impressions, and auditing compliance with this specification and other standards.

(2) Detecting security incidents, protecting against malicious, deceptive, fraudulent, or illegal activity, and prosecuting those responsible for that activity.

(3) Debugging to identify and repair errors that impair existing intended functionality.

(4) Short-term, transient use, provided the personal information that is not disclosed to another third party and is not used to build a profile about a consumer or otherwise alter an individual consumer's experience outside the current interaction, including, but not limited to, the contextual customization of ads shown as part of the same interaction.

(5) Performing services on behalf of the business or service provider, including maintaining or servicing accounts, providing customer service, processing or fulfilling orders and transactions, verifying customer information, processing payments, providing financing, providing advertising or marketing services, providing analytic services, or providing similar services on behalf of the business or service provider.

(6) Undertaking internal research for technological development and demonstration.

(7) Undertaking activities to verify or maintain the quality or safety of a service or device that is owned, manufactured, manufactured for, or controlled by the business, and to improve, upgrade, or enhance the service or device that is owned, manufactured, manufactured for, or controlled by the business.

(e) "Collects," "collected," or "collection" means buying, renting, gathering, obtaining, receiving, or accessing any personal information pertaining to a consumer by any means. This includes receiving information from the consumer, either actively or passively, or by observing the consumer's behavior.

(f) "Commercial purposes" means to advance a person's commercial or economic interests, such as by inducing another person to buy, rent, lease, join, subscribe to, provide, or exchange products, goods, property, information, or services, or enabling or effecting, directly or indirectly, a commercial transaction. "Commercial purposes" do not include for the purpose of engaging in speech that state or federal courts have recognized as noncommercial speech, including political speech and journalism.

(g) "Consumer" means a natural person who is a California resident, as defined in Section 17014 of Title 18 of the California Code of Regulations, as that section read on September 1, 2017, however identified, including by any unique identifier.

(h) "Deidentified" means information that cannot reasonably identify, relate to, describe, be capable of being associated with, or be linked, directly or indirectly, to a particular consumer, provided that a business that uses deidentified information:

(1) Has implemented technical safeguards that prohibit reidentification of the consumer to whom the information may pertain.

(2) Has implemented business processes that specifically prohibit reidentification of the information.

(3) Has implemented business processes to prevent inadvertent release of deidentified information.

(4) Makes no attempt to reidentify the information.

(i) "Designated methods for submitting requests" means a mailing address, email address, Internet Web page, Internet Web portal, toll-free telephone number, or other applicable contact information, whereby consumers may submit a request or direction under this title, and any new, consumer-friendly means of contacting a business, as approved by the Attorney General pursuant to Section 1798.185.

(j) "Device" means any physical object that is capable of connecting to the Internet, directly or indirectly, or to another device.

(k) "Health insurance information" means a consumer's insurance policy number or subscriber identification number, any unique identifier used by a health insurer to identify the consumer, or any information in the consumer's application and claims history, including any appeals records, if the information is linked or reasonably linkable to a consumer or household, including via a device, by a business or service provider.

(l) "Homepage" means the introductory page of an Internet Web site and any Internet Web page where personal information is collected. In the case of an online service, such as a mobile application, homepage means the application's platform page or download page, a link within the application, such as from the application configuration, "About," "Information," or settings page, and any other location that allows consumers to review the notice required by subdivision (a) of Section 1798.145, including, but not limited to, before downloading the application.

(m) "Infer" or "inference" means the derivation of information, data, assumptions, or conclusions from facts, evidence, or another source of information or data.

(n) "Person" means an individual, proprietorship, firm, partnership, joint venture, syndicate, business trust, company, corporation, limited liability company, association, committee, and any other organization or group of persons acting in concert.

(o)

(1) "Personal information" means information that identifies, relates to, describes, is capable of being associated with, or could reasonably be linked, directly or indirectly, with a particular consumer or household. Personal information includes, but is not limited to, the following if it identifies, relates to, describes, is capable of being associated with, or could be reasonably linked, directly or indirectly, with a particular consumer or household:

(A) Identifiers such as a real name, alias, postal address, unique personal identifier, online identifier, Internet Protocol address, email address, account name, social security number, driver's license number, passport number, or other similar identifiers.

(B) Any categories of personal information described in subdivision (e) of Section 1798.80.

(C) Characteristics of protected classifications under California or federal law.

(D) Commercial information, including records of personal property, products or services purchased, obtained, or considered, or other purchasing or consuming histories or tendencies.

(E) Biometric information.

(F) Internet or other electronic network activity information, including, but not limited to, browsing history, search history, and information regarding a consumer's interaction with an Internet Web site, application, or advertisement.

(G) Geolocation data.

(H) Audio, electronic, visual, thermal, olfactory, or similar information.

(I) Professional or employment-related information.

(J) Education information, defined as information that is not publicly available personally identifiable information as defined in the Family Educational Rights and Privacy Act (20 U.S.C. section 1232g, 34 C.F.R. Part 99).

(K) Inferences drawn from any of the information identified in this subdivision to create a profile about a consumer reflecting the consumer's preferences, characteristics, psychological trends, predispositions, behavior, attitudes, intelligence, abilities, and aptitudes.

(2) "Personal information" does not include publicly available information. For these purposes, "publicly available" means information that is lawfully made available from federal, state, or local government records, if any conditions associated with such information. "Publicly available" does not mean biometric information collected by a business about a consumer without the consumer's knowledge. Information is not "publicly available" if that data is used for a purpose that is not compatible with the purpose for which the data is maintained and made available in the government records or for which it is publicly maintained. "Publicly available" does not include consumer information that is deidentified or aggregate consumer information.

(p) "Probabilistic identifier" means the identification of a consumer or a device to a degree of certainty of more probable than not based on any categories of personal information included in, or similar to, the categories enumerated in the definition of personal information.

(q) "Processing" means any operation or set of operations that are performed on personal data or on sets of personal data, whether or not by automated means.

(r) "Pseudonymize" or "Pseudonymization" means the processing of personal information in a manner that renders the personal information no longer attributable to a specific consumer without the use of additional information, provided that the additional information is kept separately and is subject to technical and organizational measures to ensure that the personal information is not attributed to an identified or identifiable consumer.

(s) "Research" means scientific, systematic study and observation, including basic research or applied research that is in the public interest and that adheres to all other applicable ethics and privacy laws or studies conducted in the public interest in the area of public health. Research with personal information that may have been collected from a consumer in the course of the consumer's interactions with a business's service or device for other purposes shall be:

(1) Compatible with the business purpose for which the personal information was collected.

(2) Subsequently pseudonymized and deidentified, or deidentified and in the aggregate, such that the information cannot reasonably identify, relate to, describe, be capable of being associated with, or be linked, directly or indirectly, to a particular consumer.

(3) Made subject to technical safeguards that prohibit reidentification of the consumer to whom the information may pertain.

(4) Subject to business processes that specifically prohibit reidentification of the information.

(5) Made subject to business processes to prevent inadvertent release of deidentified information.

(6) Protected from any reidentification attempts.

(7) Used solely for research purposes that are compatible with the context in which the personal information was collected.

(8) Not be used for any commercial purpose.

(9) Subjected by the business conducting the research to additional security controls limit access to the research data to only those individuals in a business as are necessary to carry out the research purpose.

(t)

(1) "Sell," "selling," "sale," or "sold," means selling, renting, releasing, disclosing, disseminating, making available, transferring, or otherwise communicating orally, in writing, or by electronic or other means, a consumer's personal information by the business to another business or a third party for monetary or other valuable consideration.

(2) For purposes of this title, a business does not sell personal information when:

(A) A consumer uses or directs the business to intentionally disclose personal information or uses the business to intentionally interact with a third party, provided the third party does not also sell the personal information, unless that disclosure would be consistent with the provisions of this title. An intentional interaction occurs when the consumer intends to interact with the third party, via one or more deliberate interactions. Hovering over, muting, pausing, or closing a given piece of content does not constitute a consumer's intent to interact with a third party.

(B) The business uses or shares an identifier for a consumer who has opted out of the sale of the consumer's personal information for the purposes of alerting third parties that the consumer has opted out of the sale of the consumer's personal information.

(C) The business uses or shares with a service provider personal information of a consumer that is necessary to perform a business purpose if both of the following conditions are met:

(i) The business has provided notice that information being used or shared in its terms and conditions consistent with Section 1798.135.

(ii) The service provider does not further collect, sell, or use the personal information of the consumer except as necessary to perform the business purpose.

(D) The business transfers to a third party the personal information of a consumer as an asset that is part of a merger, acquisition, bankruptcy, or other transaction in which the third party assumes control of all or part of the business, provided that information is used or shared consistently with Sections 1798.110 and 1798.115. If a third party materially alters how it uses or shares the personal information of a consumer in a manner that is materially inconsistent with the promises made at the time of collection, it shall provide prior notice of the new or changed practice to the consumer. The notice shall be sufficiently prominent and robust to ensure that existing consumers can easily exercise their choices consistently with Section 1798.120. This subparagraph does not authorize a business to make material, retroactive privacy policy changes or make other changes in their privacy policy in a manner that would violate the Unfair and Deceptive Practices Act (Chapter 5 (commencing with Section 17200) of Part 2 of Division 7 of the Business and Professions Code).

(u) "Service" or "services" means work, labor, and services, including services furnished in connection with the sale or repair of goods.

(v) "Service provider" means a sole proprietorship, partnership, limited liability company, corporation, association, or other legal entity that is organized or operated for the profit or financial benefit of its shareholders or other owners, that processes information on behalf of a business and to which the business discloses a consumer's personal information for a business purpose pursuant to a written contract, provided that the contract prohibits the entity receiving the information from retaining, using, or disclosing the personal information for any purpose other than for the specific purpose of performing the services specified in the contract for the business, or as otherwise permitted by this title, including retaining, using, or disclosing the personal information for a commercial purpose other than providing the services specified in the contract with the business.

(w) "Third party" means a person who is not any of the following:

(1) The business that collects personal information from consumers under this title.

(2)

(A) A person to whom the business discloses a consumer's personal information for a business purpose pursuant to a written contract, provided that the contract:

(i) Prohibits the person receiving the personal information from:

(I) Selling the personal information.

(II) Retaining, using, or disclosing the personal information for any purpose other than for the specific purpose of performing the services specified in the contract, including retaining, using, or disclosing the personal information for a commercial purpose other than providing the services specified in the contract.

(III) Retaining, using, or disclosing the information outside of the direct business relationship between the person and the business.

(ii) Includes a certification made by the person receiving the personal information that the person understands the restrictions in subparagraph (A) and will comply with them.

(B) A person covered by this paragraph that violates any of the restrictions set forth in this title shall be liable for the violations. A business that discloses personal information to a person covered by this paragraph in compliance with this paragraph shall not be liable under this title if the person receiving the personal information uses it in violation of the restrictions set forth in this title, provided that, at the time of disclosing the personal information, the business does not have actual knowledge, or reason to believe, that the person intends to commit such a violation.

(x) "Unique identifier" or "Unique personal identifier" means a persistent identifier that can be used to recognize a consumer, a family, or a device that is linked to a consumer or family, over time and across different services, including, but not limited to, a device identifier; an Internet Protocol address; cookies, beacons, pixel tags, mobile ad identifiers, or similar technology; customer number, unique pseudonym, or user alias; telephone numbers, or other forms of persistent or probabilistic identifiers that can be used to identify a particular consumer or device. For purposes of this subdivision, "family" means a custodial parent or guardian and any minor children over which the parent or guardian has custody.

(y) "Verifiable consumer request" means a request that is made by a consumer, by a consumer on behalf of the consumer's minor child, or by a natural person or a person registered with the Secretary of State, authorized by the consumer to act on the consumer's behalf, and that the business can reasonably verify, pursuant to regulations adopted by the Attorney General pursuant to paragraph (7) of subdivision (a) of Section 1798.185 to be the consumer about whom the business has collected personal information. A business is not obligated to provide information to the consumer pursuant to Sections 1798.110 and 1798.115 if the business cannot verify, pursuant this subdivision and regulations adopted by the Attorney General pursuant to paragraph (7) of subdivision (a) of Section 1798.185, that the consumer making the request is the consumer about whom the business has collected information or is a person authorized by the consumer to act on such consumer's behalf.

(Amended (as added by Stats. 2018, Ch. 55, Sec. 3) by Stats. 2018, Ch. 735, Sec. 9. (SB 1121) Effective September 23, 2018. Section operative January 1, 2020, pursuant to Section 1798.198.)

1798.145.

(a) The obligations imposed on businesses by this title shall not restrict a business's ability to:

(1) Comply with federal, state, or local laws.

(2) Comply with a civil, criminal, or regulatory inquiry, investigation, subpoena, or summons by federal, state, or local authorities.

(3) Cooperate with law enforcement agencies concerning conduct or activity that the business, service provider, or third party reasonably and in

good faith believes may violate federal, state, or local law.

(4) Exercise or defend legal claims.

(5) Collect, use, retain, sell, or disclose consumer information that is deidentified or in the aggregate consumer information.

(6) Collect or sell a consumer's personal information if every aspect of that commercial conduct takes place wholly outside of California. For purposes of this title, commercial conduct takes place wholly outside of California if the business collected that information while the consumer was outside of California, no part of the sale of the consumer's personal information occurred in California, and no personal information collected while the consumer was in California is sold. This paragraph shall not permit a business from storing, including on a device, personal information about a consumer when the consumer is in California and then collecting that personal information when the consumer and stored personal information is outside of California.

(b) The obligations imposed on businesses by Sections 1798.110 to 1798.135, inclusive, shall not apply where compliance by the business with the title would violate an evidentiary privilege under California law and shall not prevent a business from providing the personal information of a consumer to a person covered by an evidentiary privilege under California law as part of a privileged communication.

(c)

(1) This title shall not apply to any of the following:

(A) Medical information governed by the Confidentiality of Medical Information Act (Part 2.6 (commencing with Section 56) of Division 1) or protected health information that is collected by a covered entity or business associate governed by the privacy, security, and breach notification rules issued by the United States Department of Health and Human Services, Parts 160 and 164 of Title 45 of the Code of Federal Regulations, established pursuant to the Health Insurance Portability and Accountability Act of 1996 (Public Law 104-191) and the Health Information Technology for Economic and Clinical Health Act (Public Law 111-5).

(B) A provider of health care governed by the Confidentiality of Medical Information Act (Part 2.6 (commencing with Section 56) of Division 1) or a covered entity governed by the privacy, security, and breach notification rules issued by the United States Department of Health and Human Services, Parts 160 and 164 of Title 45 of the Code of Federal Regulations, established pursuant to the Health Insurance Portability and Accountability Act of 1996 (Public Law 104-191), to the extent the provider or covered entity maintains patient information in the same manner as medical information or protected health information as described in subparagraph (A) of this section.

(C) Information collected as part of a clinical trial subject to the Federal Policy for the Protection of Human Subjects, also known as the

Common Rule, pursuant to good clinical practice guidelines issued by the International Council for Harmonisation or pursuant to human subject protection requirements of the United States Food and Drug Administration.

(2) For purposes of this subdivision, the definitions of "medical information" and "provider of health care" in Section 56.05 shall apply and the definitions of "business associate," "covered entity," and "protected health information" in Section 160.103 of Title 45 of the Code of Federal Regulations shall apply.

(d) This title shall not apply to the sale of personal information to or from a consumer reporting agency if that information is to be reported in, or used to generate, a consumer report as defined by subdivision (d) of Section 1681a of Title 15 of the United States Code, and use of that information is limited by the federal Fair Credit Reporting Act (15 U.S.C. Sec. 1681 et seq.).

(e) This title shall not apply to personal information collected, processed, sold, or disclosed pursuant to the federal Gramm-Leach-Bliley Act (Public Law 106-102), and implementing regulations, or the California Financial Information Privacy Act (Division 1.4 (commencing with Section 4050) of the Financial Code). This subdivision shall not apply to Section 1798.150.

(f) This title shall not apply to personal information collected, processed, sold, or disclosed pursuant to the Driver's Privacy Protection Act of 1994 (18 U.S.C. Sec. 2721 et seq.). This subdivision shall not apply to Section 1798.150.

(g) Notwithstanding a business's obligations to respond to and honor consumer rights requests pursuant to this title:

(1) A time period for a business to respond to any verified consumer request may be extended by up to 90 additional days where necessary, taking into account the complexity and number of the requests. The business shall inform the consumer of any such extension within 45 days of receipt of the request, together with the reasons for the delay.

(2) If the business does not take action on the request of the consumer, the business shall inform the consumer, without delay and at the latest within the time period permitted of response by this section, of the reasons for not taking action and any rights the consumer may have to appeal the decision to the business.

(3) If requests from a consumer are manifestly unfounded or excessive, in particular because of their repetitive character, a business may either charge a reasonable fee, taking into account the administrative costs of providing the information or communication or taking the action requested, or refuse to act on the request and notify the consumer of the reason for refusing the request. The business shall bear the burden of demonstrating that any verified consumer request is manifestly unfounded or excessive.

(h) A business that discloses personal information to a service provider shall not be liable under this title if the service provider receiving the personal information uses it in violation of the restrictions set forth in the title, provided that, at the time of disclosing the personal information, the business does not have actual knowledge, or reason to believe, that the service provider intends to commit such a violation. A service provider shall likewise not be liable under this title for the obligations of a business for which it provides services as set forth in this title.

(i) This title shall not be construed to require a business to reidentify or otherwise link information that is not maintained in a manner that would be considered personal information.

(j) The rights afforded to consumers and the obligations imposed on the business in this title shall not adversely affect the rights and freedoms of other consumers.

(k) The rights afforded to consumers and the obligations imposed on any business under this title shall not apply to the extent that they infringe on the noncommercial activities of a person or entity described in subdivision (b) of Section 2 of Article I of the California Constitution.

(Amended (as added by Stats. 2018, Ch. 55, Sec. 3) by Stats. 2018, Ch. 735, Sec. 10. (SB 1121) Effective September 23, 2018. Section operative January 1, 2020, pursuant to Section 1798.198.)

1798.150.

(a)

(1) Any consumer whose nonencrypted or nonredacted personal information, as defined in subparagraph (A) of paragraph (1) of subdivision (d) of Section 1798.81.5, is subject to an unauthorized access and exfiltration, theft, or disclosure as a result of the business's violation of the duty to implement and

maintain reasonable security procedures and practices appropriate to the nature of the information to protect the personal information may institute a civil action for any of the following:

(A) To recover damages in an amount not less than one hundred dollars ($100) and not greater than seven hundred and fifty ($750) per consumer per incident or actual damages, whichever is greater.

(B) Injunctive or declaratory relief.

(C) Any other relief the court deems proper.

(2) In assessing the amount of statutory damages, the court shall consider any one or more of the relevant circumstances presented by any of the parties to the case, including, but not limited to, the nature and seriousness of the misconduct, the number of violations, the persistence of the misconduct, the length of time over which the misconduct occurred, the willfulness of the defendant's misconduct, and the defendant's assets, liabilities, and net worth.

(b) Actions pursuant to this section may be brought by a consumer if, prior to initiating any action against a business for statutory damages on an individual or class-wide basis, a consumer provides a business 30 days' written notice identifying the specific provisions of this title the consumer alleges have been or are being violated. In the event a cure is possible, if within the 30 days the business actually cures the noticed violation and provides the consumer an express written statement that the violations have been cured and that no further violations shall occur, no action for individual statutory damages or class-wide statutory damages may be initiated against the business. No notice shall be required prior to an individual consumer initiating an action solely for actual pecuniary damages suffered as a result of the alleged violations of this title. If a business continues to violate this title in breach of the express written statement provided to the consumer under this section, the consumer may initiate an action against the business to enforce the written statement and may pursue statutory damages for each breach of the express written statement, as well as any other violation of the title that postdates the written statement.

(c) The cause of action established by this section shall apply only to violations as defined in subdivision (a) and shall not be based on violations of any other section of this title. Nothing in this title shall be interpreted to serve as the basis for a private right of action under any other law. This shall not be construed to relieve any party from any duties or obligations imposed under other law or the United States or California Constitution.

(Amended (as added by Stats. 2018, Ch. 55, Sec. 3) by Stats. 2018, Ch. 735, Sec. 11. (SB 1121) Effective September 23, 2018. Section operative January 1, 2020, pursuant to Section 1798.198.)

1798.155.

(a) Any business or third party may seek the opinion of the Attorney General for guidance on how to comply with the provisions of this title.

(b) A business shall be in violation of this title if it fails to cure any alleged violation within 30 days after being notified of alleged noncompliance. Any business, service provider, or other person that violates this title shall be subject to an injunction and liable for a civil penalty of not more than two thousand five hundred dollars ($2,500) for each violation or seven thousand five hundred dollars ($7,500) for each intentional violation, which shall be assessed and recovered in a civil action brought in the name of the people of the State of California by the Attorney General. The civil penalties provided for in this section shall be exclusively assessed and recovered in a civil action brought in the name of the people of the State of California by the Attorney General.

(c) Any civil penalty assessed for a violation of this title, and the proceeds of any settlement of an action brought pursuant to subdivision (b), shall be deposited in the Consumer Privacy Fund, created within the General Fund pursuant to subdivision (a) of Section 1798.160 with the intent to fully offset any costs incurred by the state courts and the Attorney General in connection with this title.

(Amended (as added by Stats. 2018, Ch. 55, Sec. 3) by Stats. 2018, Ch. 735, Sec. 12. (SB 1121) Effective September 23, 2018. Section operative January 1, 2020, pursuant to Section 1798.198.)

1798.160.

(a) A special fund to be known as the "Consumer Privacy Fund" is hereby created within the General Fund in the State Treasury, and is available upon appropriation by the Legislature to offset any costs incurred by the state courts in connection with actions brought to enforce this title and any costs incurred by the Attorney General in carrying out the Attorney General's duties under this title.

(b) Funds transferred to the Consumer Privacy Fund shall be used exclusively to offset any costs incurred by the state courts and the Attorney General in connection with this title. These funds shall not be subject to appropriation or transfer by the Legislature for any other purpose, unless the Director of Finance determines that the funds are in excess of the funding needed to fully offset the costs incurred by the state courts and the Attorney General in connection with this title, in which case the Legislature may appropriate excess funds for other purposes.

(Added by Stats. 2018, Ch. 55, Sec. 3. (AB 375) Effective January 1, 2019. Section operative January 1, 2020, pursuant to Section 1798.198.)

1798.175.

This title is intended to further the constitutional right of privacy and to supplement existing laws relating to consumers' personal information, including, but not limited to, Chapter 22 (commencing with Section 22575) of Division 8 of the Business and Professions Code and Title 1.81 (commencing with Section 1798.80). The provisions of this title are not limited to information collected electronically or over the Internet, but apply to the collection and sale of all personal information collected by a business from consumers. Wherever possible, law relating to consumers' personal information should be construed to harmonize with the provisions of this title, but in the event of a conflict between other laws and the provisions of this title, the provisions of the law that afford the greatest protection for the right of privacy for consumers shall control.

(Added by Stats. 2018, Ch. 55, Sec. 3. (AB 375) Effective January 1, 2019. Section operative January 1, 2020, pursuant to Section 1798.198.)

1798.180.

This title is a matter of statewide concern and supersedes and preempts all rules, regulations, codes, ordinances, and other laws adopted by a city, county, city and county, municipality, or local agency regarding the collection and sale of consumers' personal information by a business.

(Added by Stats. 2018, Ch. 55, Sec. 3. (AB 375) Effective January 1, 2019. Section operative September 23, 2018, pursuant to Section 1798.199.)

1798.185.

(a) On or before July 1, 2020, the Attorney General shall solicit broad public participation and adopt regulations to further the purposes of this title, including, but not limited to, the following areas:

(1) Updating as needed additional categories of personal information to those enumerated in subdivision (c) of Section 1798.130 and subdivision (o) of Section 1798.140 in order to address changes in technology, data collection practices, obstacles to implementation, and privacy concerns.

(2) Updating as needed the definition of unique identifiers to address changes in technology, data collection, obstacles to implementation, and privacy concerns, and additional categories to the definition

of designated methods for submitting requests to facilitate a consumer's ability to obtain information from a business pursuant to Section 1798.130.

(3) Establishing any exceptions necessary to comply with state or federal law, including, but not limited to, those relating to trade secrets and intellectual property rights, within one year of passage of this title and as needed thereafter.

(4) Establishing rules and procedures for the following:

   (A) To facilitate and govern the submission of a request by a consumer to opt-out of the sale of personal information pursuant to paragraph (1) of subdivision (a) of Section 1798.145.

   (B) To govern business compliance with a consumer's opt-out request.

   (C) For the development and use of a recognizable and uniform opt-out logo or button by all businesses to promote consumer awareness of the opportunity to opt-out of the sale of personal information.

(5) Adjusting the monetary threshold in subparagraph (A) of paragraph (1) of subdivision (c) of Section 1798.140 in January of every odd-numbered year to reflect any increase in the Consumer Price Index.

(6) Establishing rules, procedures, and any exceptions necessary to ensure that the notices and information that businesses are required to provide pursuant to this title are provided in a manner that may be easily understood by the average consumer, are accessible to consumers with disabilities, and are available in

the language primarily used to interact with the consumer, including establishing rules and guidelines regarding financial incentive offerings, within one year of passage of this title and as needed thereafter.

(7) Establishing rules and procedures to further the purposes of Sections 1798.110 and 1798.115 and to facilitate a consumer's or the consumer's authorized agent's ability to obtain information pursuant to Section 1798.130, with the goal of minimizing the administrative burden on consumers, taking into account available technology, security concerns, and the burden on the business, to govern a business's determination that a request for information received by a consumer is a verifiable consumer request, including treating a request submitted through a password-protected account maintained by the consumer with the business while the consumer is logged into the account as a verifiable consumer request and providing a mechanism for a consumer who does not maintain an account with the business to request information through the business's authentication of the consumer's identity, within one year of passage of this title and as needed thereafter.

(b) The Attorney General may adopt additional regulations as necessary to further the purposes of this title.

(c) The Attorney General shall not bring an enforcement action under this title until six months after the publication of the final regulations issued pursuant to this section or July 1, 2020, whichever is sooner.

(Amended (as added by Stats. 2018, Ch. 55, Sec. 3) by Stats. 2018, Ch. 735, Sec. 13. (SB 1121) Effective September 23,

2018. Section operative January 1, 2020, pursuant to Section 1798.198.)

1798.190.

If a series of steps or transactions were component parts of a single transaction intended from the beginning to be taken with the intention of avoiding the reach of this title, including the disclosure of information by a business to a third party in order to avoid the definition of sell, a court shall disregard the intermediate steps or transactions for purposes of effectuating the purposes of this title.

(Added by Stats. 2018, Ch. 55, Sec. 3. (AB 375) Effective January 1, 2019. Section operative January 1, 2020, pursuant to Section 1798.198.)

1798.192.

Any provision of a contract or agreement of any kind that purports to waive or limit in any way a consumer's rights under this title, including, but not limited to, any right to a remedy or means of enforcement, shall be deemed contrary to public policy and shall be void and unenforceable. This section shall not prevent a consumer from declining to request information from a business, declining to opt-out of a business's sale of the consumer's personal information, or authorizing a business to sell the consumer's personal information after previously opting out.

(Amended (as added by Stats. 2018, Ch. 55, Sec. 3) by Stats. 2018, Ch. 735, Sec. 14. (SB 1121) Effective September 23, 2018. Section operative January 1, 2020, pursuant to Section 1798.198.)

1798.194.

This title shall be liberally construed to effectuate its purposes.

(Added by Stats. 2018, Ch. 55, Sec. 3. (AB 375) Effective January 1, 2019. Section operative January 1, 2020, pursuant to Section 1798.198.)

1798.196.

This title is intended to supplement federal and state law, if permissible, but shall not apply if such application is preempted by, or in conflict with, federal law or the United States or California Constitution.

(Amended (as added by Stats. 2018, Ch. 55, Sec. 3) by Stats. 2018, Ch. 735, Sec. 15. (SB 1121) Effective September 23, 2018. Section operative January 1, 2020, pursuant to Section 1798.198.)

1798.198.

(a) Subject to limitation provided in subdivision (b), and in Section 1798.199, this title shall be operative January 1, 2020.

(b) This title shall become operative only if initiative measure No. 17-0039, The Consumer Right to Privacy Act of 2018, is withdrawn from the ballot pursuant to Section 9604 of the Elections Code.

(Amended (as added by Stats. 2018, Ch. 55, Sec. 3) by Stats. 2018, Ch. 735, Sec. 16. (SB 1121) Effective September 23, 2018.)

1798.199.

Notwithstanding Section 1798.198, Section 1798.180 shall be operative on the effective date of the act adding this section.

(Added by Stats. 2018, Ch. 735, Sec. 17. (SB 1121) Effective September 23, 2018. Operative September 23, 2018)

FURTHER READING

IT Governance Publishing (ITGP) is the world's leading publisher for governance and compliance. Our industry-leading pocket guides, books, training resources, and toolkits are written by real-world practitioners and thought leaders. They are used globally by audiences of all levels, from students to C-suite executives.

Our high-quality publications cover all IT governance, risk, and compliance frameworks, and are available in a range of formats. This ensures our customers can access the information they need in the way they need it.

Other resources you may find useful include:

- *EU GDPR – A pocket guide, second edition* by Alan Calder, *www.itgovernancepublishing.co.uk/product/eu-gdpr-a-pocket-guide-second-edition*
- *EU GDPR – A pocket guide (European), second edition* by Alan Calder, *www.itgovernancepublishing.co.uk/product/eu-gdpr-a-pocket-guide-european-second-edition*
- *EU General Data Protection Regulation (GDPR) Documentation Toolkit v2.0*, *www.itgovernancepublishing.co.uk/product/eu-general-data-protection-regulation-gdpr-documentation-toolkit-v2-0*

For more information on ITGP and branded publishing services, and to view our full list of publications, visit *www.itgovernancepublishing.co.uk*.

Further reading

To receive regular updates from ITGP, including information on new publications in your area(s) of interest, sign up for our newsletter at *www.itgovernancepublishing.co.uk/topic/newsletter*.

Branded publishing

Through our branded publishing service, you can customize ITGP publications with your organization's branding.

Find out more at *www.itgovernancepublishing.co.uk/topic/branded-publishing-services*.

Related services

ITGP is part of GRC International Group, which offers a comprehensive range of complementary products and services to help organizations meet their objectives.

For a full range of resources on the CCPA visit *www.itgovernanceusa.com/california-consumer-privacy*.

Training services

The IT Governance training program is built on our extensive practical experience designing and implementing management systems based on ISO standards, best practice, and regulations.

Our courses help attendees develop practical skills and comply with contractual and regulatory requirements. They also support career development via recognized qualifications.

Further reading

Learn more about our training courses in data protection and view the full course catalog at *www.itgovernanceusa.com/training*.

Professional services and consultancy

We are a leading global consultancy of IT governance, risk management, and compliance solutions. We advise organizations around the world on their most critical issues, and present cost-saving and risk-reducing solutions based on international best practice and frameworks.

We offer a wide range of delivery methods to suit all budgets, timescales, and preferred project approaches.

Find out how our consultancy services can help your organization at *www.itgovernanceusa.com/consulting*.

Industry news

Want to stay up to date with the latest developments and resources in the IT governance and compliance market? Subscribe to our Daily Sentinel newsletter and we will send you mobile-friendly emails with fresh news and features about your preferred areas of interest, as well as unmissable offers and free resources to help you successfully start your projects. *www.itgovernanceusa.com/daily-sentinel*.

Lightning Source UK Ltd.
Milton Keynes UK
UKHW022018110220
358552UK00015B/217